An
Amazing
Journey

Susan F. Bailess

savage
PRESS
A Superior Publishing Company

P.O. Box 115 • Superior, WI 54880
(218) 391-3070 • www.savpress.com

First Edition

Cover design: Dezime Graphics
Cover photo: Ted Thompson, Duluth Camera Exchange

ISBN-978-1-937706-16-1

Library of Congress Catalog Card Number: 2016944627

Published by:

Savage Press
P.O. Box 115
Superior, WI 54880

Phone: 218-391-3070
Email: mail@savpress.com
Website: www.savpress.com

Printed in the United States of America

An Amazing Journey

C. E. Hanning's Autobiography

Completed 1916

CHARLES ELISHA HANNING

Edited By

Susan F. Bailess

ACKNOWLEDGMENTS

I would like to thank these people who have been very helpful while I was writing the text of this book. Thanks to Debbie, Mike, Amy, and my sister Betty, and brother-in-law, Bernie. Thank you Glenna, Barry, Janice, Charlene, Becky and Ernie for the information given me about your growing families. Many thanks to Ted for the lovely cover picture of the U.S. Brig Niagara sailing on Lake Superior.

— Susan

DEDICATION

While working on Charles' book, I could not help but reflect on a day many years ago when my mother started typing this story. After about a week trying to put Grandfather's story together, and getting only three pages typed, she said to me, "Susan, I cannot make head or tails out of what he is trying to say. Somehow his life's adventures should be preserved, but I just can't do it."

I dedicate this book in memory to my mother and father, Janey Carr Bailess and Andrew Bailess. In addition I dedicate it to all of the descendants of Charles Hanning who have passed away, to those living, and to all who will follow.

Jane "Janey" Carr Bailess   *Andrew "Andy" R. Bailess*

INTRODUCTION

I hope you will enjoy reading about one man's life back in the eighteen hundreds. Laugh and have a good time reading Charles' handwritten autobiography. I am not sure there needs to be much clarification about the information written in this book, but the following will hopefully answer any questions you might have. It has been quite an adventure untangling Charles' life.

While writing about his life, I found that Charles wrote his thoughts in both past and present tense. Some of these situations have been changed for clarification and others have remained as he wrote them.

His travels around the world are probably not precisely in the order they were taken. However, I think most all of them are in with one exception. That was a short trip he took to Hampton Roads, a southwest seaport in the state of Virginia, before leaving for California.

All locations on maps are only approximate.

In the era in which he lived, dinner refers to lunch and supper is dinner.

Any information in parenthesis is included to provide more information.

I took the liberty to put his writing into conversational text to add interest to his adventures.

To write a smooth transition from one subject to another, I added text or changed the wording for an easy flow and transition.

The original Bidwell Bar Suspension Bridge that Charles worked on in Oroville, California, is registered as a Historical Landmark.

The dates of the Civil War battles were taken from many different sources for accuracy of the areas he fought in. He used his middle name, Elisha, during his service.

In the genealogy section, White River Junction, Vermont is like a suburb of Hartford, Vermont.

A photo in the chapter "Childhood Years" cannot be accurately identified as I was unable to find the original. Using the information I had is the reason for the caption. Another possibility is; Almon Shepherd, his mother Jessie, and his sister Sybil.

The section in Charles' book about the Wareham Council meeting was only summarized due to its lengthy discussion.

— Susan

Table of Contents

Charles Elisha Hanning family photo taken around 1910.
Back row, Janey Carr, Ernest Shephard, Charles Shepherd, Agnes Carr.
Front row, Ellen E. Hanning, Almon Shepherd, Charles Elisha Hanning,
Sybil Shepherd, Jessie Shepherd

CHILDHOOD YEARS 1830 - 1843

This is a sketch of my life, Charles Elisha Hanning, written by myself who is almost seventy-nine years old. (Charles started this autobiography in 1908.)

I was born in Portland, Maine, the twenty-fifth day of May 1830. Before I was born, Deb and John, my mother and father lived on a farm with my father's family in Old Town, Maine. Father was going to go to sea as a shipmaster in a ship that was built for him in Portland, and Mother went there to stay with her folks to be with him. When he got ready to sail she had to stay there until I arrived. There were no steamers running from Portland to Bangor, about three miles from Old Town, and she had to go to Bangor in a sailing vessel when I was three months old. I suppose that is why I was a sailor.

My father had accumulated quite a fortune for those days, and he retired from foreign voyages when I was two and a half years old. He went in lumbering and real estate, and he became very poor. He lost all the money he had saved, the house and property he owned, and the investments he had in navigation. He had to go to sea again, but this time he went coasting.

It was about the time I should have gone to school, but in those days they did not have free schools, and my father could not afford to send me. I was really sad too, because most of my good friends were able to go and I couldn't. It was quite unfortunate, because even though I found boys to play with who were not in school, I couldn't say they were good friends. They saw no need to go school. When we were together I would suggest we play games or ball in the park, but that wasn't exciting enough. So off we would go to do what they wanted to do, and it often ended in our getting into trouble.

They loved going to the candy store, distracting the salesperson, and see how much candy and gum they could walk off with. I was brought up to be honest, and I never did take anything, but I was an accomplice. When Mother found out about what was going on, I was in for a long talking to. I was no longer allowed to play with them. Luckily school was out about noon each day, and Mother kept me busy until my friends came to call for me in the afternoon. Then we had some good clean fun. During the morning, Mother would work with me for several hours teaching me reading, writing, and how to add and subtract. After my lessons were done, I would help mother around the house with work that needed to be done. I would do anything she asked me to do, because I wanted to stay out of trouble.

I did everything I could to earn money. I was a pretty big robust kid, and those that hired me thought I was older than I was. When I was ten years old, I worked and bought myself the first pair of boots I ever had. I tell you I was one proud boy. When I got any money, I would give it to my mother for I loved her, and I love to think of her.

When I was in my ninth year, the United States and England had trouble about the boundary line between Maine and New Brunswick. Maine wanted much of the area north of the St. John River, and New

Brunswick wanted land south of it. Both countries wanted control of the river for trade purposes. (The boundary line set by the treaty closely follows the Saint John River with its beginning in northwestern Maine near eastern Quebec. The river flows northeasterly up and around northern Maine where it boarders New Brunswick. It continues flowing southerly between these two countries until reaching Grand Falls. It then veers southeasterly entirely in New Brunswick until it flows into the Bay of Fundy at Saint John. This was known as the Aroostook War from February to May 1839. It resulted in a peaceful settlement known as the Webster-Ashton Treaty of 1842.) [1]

This map gives the approximate location of the settlement of boundaries set by the Webster-Ashton treaty after the Aroostook War, the flow of the Saint John River, and the southern, rugged coastline of Maine where Charles grew up.

Troops were sent to the boundary area when a war cloud arose, but fortunately they were not needed. The men negotiating the boundary lines reached a decision that both countries agreed on, and the troops were sent home. My father did teaming for the government, and he was asked to go and bring back supplies that had been sent with the troops. When I found out he was going, I coaxed Father, "Please let me go with you and help drive one of the teams back to Bangor." He was a little hesitant at first, but after talking to mother he consented to taking me with him.

Everywhere we stopped, every public house, the soldiers and the women folk went crazy over me. Father could not do anything about this situation, as they would not allow him any control over me. He told me, "I will settle with you when we get home," but he never did. We were gone three and a half days. The first night where we stopped the ladies made a uniform for me, the soldiers made a sword, and the girls made a scabbard. They put epaulets on my shoulders, and I was a full-fledged captain. The soldiers that saw me after that always called me the young captain. When we got back home, one of the Sergeants let me have his horse to ride into the village. I rode along side the General, and the folks at the public house went wild.

Father told me, "You better go home and see your mother right now."

They sent for her about a mile away, and when she saw me in uniform she wanted to know what they had been doing to her child. She took me up in her arms and sat down.

I told her, "Mama, you ought not make a baby of me for I am captain."

Then I went home with her, and everybody in the place was running to see me.

One woman told my mother, "I would give you my farm with the sawmill on it if he could just be mine." She was Mother's best friend.

My sisters were jealous and made fun of me for being a soldier, but we went out into the woods to have some fun. I decided to climb a tree, and when I was up in the tree they started cutting it down to scare me. When they got it almost ready to fall, and were having to hold it up so it wouldn't topple over, I started to sway it. They begged me to come down. After I had plagued them all I wanted, and they had made all kinds of promises to me, I went down but they tried to break me all up. I told Mother about it. She said, "They ought to be licked for cutting the tree down. They know they cannot scare you."

Mother and Father sent me to school shortly after the above event. I was in my tenth year, and the school teacher told Mother. "He is the sweetest scholar I have, but he is very mischievous. He is so sly I cannot punish him."

Mother told her, "Do not spare him. You must make him mind. I certainly have no trouble with that, for he better do anything that you tell him to do. He must obey you."

My teacher said, "I think if I told him to climb up on the ridge pole he would do it."

Mother told her, "Oh, he would love that. It would be just what would suit him. I have to tell you about the time he was on the roof of the barn helping his father shingle and put weatherboards on the gables. He was removing the staging boards, and his father was on the ladder putting weatherboards on one end of the gables. Evidently his father put the hammer on the ridge pole and it started to slide off, so his father yelled at him to grab it. Charles started for it, but most of the staging on that side of the roof had been removed, and there was no sure footing. I happened to be looking out of the window, and I saw him running to get the hammer before it fell on the ground. Fortunately, he caught it before it got to the edge of the roof without tumbling to the ground himself. Then he started to run around to the other side of the roof to give the hammer to his father, and I could see he didn't have any shoes on. I couldn't believe he was up there in his bare feet.

His teacher told Deb, "I'm sure you have your hands full with such a mischievous young boy like Charles, but he is a darling and he is very intelligent.

Mother didn't tell my teacher the whole story. After she spotted the 'no shoes' issue she came out to the barn and said to me, "Get down here now, and at least get shoes on your feet. You frightened me. If you had fallen I most likely would have had to use my broom and dustpan to sweep you up."

His reply was, "But, Mama, you know I have no way to get down. Father is using the only ladder we have."

His mother said, "John, I think Charles should come down and get shoes on his feet."

"He's been up here all afternoon without shoes, and we are almost done. We'll be down soon. He's doing just fine, Deb, leave him alone," said John.

"All right, I'm going back in the house and get dinner. Hurry up and be careful," Deb said. (This evidently was a saddle roof that has a steep slope to it, creating a gable at each end of the ridgepole. This is where the weatherboards, an early form of siding, were put on.)[2] We put the saddle boards on, cleared the roof off, and took the rest of the staging off. Then I took a broom and swept the roof all off before going in to supper.

Mother told me, "If you ever do anything like that again I will skin you."

I told her, "Mother, you know that would kill me."

She said, "I do not mean I'd take your hide off."

While I was going to school we got to laughing one day at a little instance I won't mention, and the teacher had to dismiss the school. I had laughed so much I got hysterical and could not stop. She wrapped her arms around me, took me home, put me to bed, and sent for my mother. We lived only a short distance from the school. I had fallen asleep when mother got home, but she had a few things to say to me when I woke up, because I was laughing again. She told me, "I think it's time for you to get hold of yourself and control this laughing. If you do not stop I will whip you." Believe you me I stopped. The next morning when I went to school we all started laughing again, and the teacher gave me a sound switching. That made me mad, but it ended our laughing jag for good. I sometimes wonder if they were mad at us, because they had no idea what all of us were laughing at, and they wanted to get in on the fun.

When the teacher dismissed the school at noon, she said to me, "Charles, I don't know what was so funny yesterday, but you kids are all old enough to know right from wrong, and now you must learn how to control your reactions when these situations arise. She put her arms around me, and we gave each other a big hug. I did not lay up anything against her, for I thought as much of her as she did of me.

The next winter I did not have a chance to go to school. That was in Old Town, Penobscot County, Maine, where my folks were living at that time. The next summer I was in my eleventh year and my father moved down on the coast to Searsport and went coasting. This time I went to find a job, so I could earn money and give it to my mother to make things easier for her. I missed not having my father around even though we didn't always agree on things.

Mother and Father had become acquainted with a Mr. and Mrs. McGilvery who had a daughter about my age. I was with them much of my spare time, as their daughter and I became good friends. We enjoyed sitting in the back yard watching birds, looking in her bird book, and reading about them. We would play cards, board games, and hide and seek in the woods behind her house. Her dog thought this was great fun and always helped find the one hiding. Every now and then her folks would invite me to dinner, and then we chatted about the things we had done that afternoon. We just enjoyed being together, and her folks were very nice to me. If they got a present for their daughter they would get something for me also. I continued finding small jobs where I could make some money and of course did chores around the house to help Mother.

Putting the pieces of a puzzle together, I strongly feel this is Charles
with his mother, Deb, and one of his sisters.
Perhaps positive identification will come to light as a result of this book.

MET CAPTAIN CHASE 1843 - 1850

I left home when I was thirteen years old as I got put out (mad) at Father. I went to Belfast about six miles from where Father lived. Both Mother and Father thought I had gone to my sister's, because that's where I went when I had any trouble with my folks. They did not look for me for about a day and a half when one of my sisters went to Mother and asked, "Mother, I haven't seen Charles for several days, and it's not like him to not check in with me. Is everything all right here?"

Mother spoke up, "What, you haven't seen him either? We just figured he was with you, because we had a squabble the other night and he got mad. Why would he do this to us? We have to find him. What should we do?"

Charles' sister said, "Well, let's start searching for him. I don't know what else to do."

They began their search for me, but all they could find out was that people down by the vessels saw a young boy going aboard a schooner with a Captain. They did not know what the schooner's name or the Captain's name was, nor did they know for sure that it was me.

When I got into Belfast, I walked down to the wharf to see what was going on. It looked like there was one captain who was getting ready to sail, so I struck up a conversation with him. After visiting for a few minutes he said to me, "I'm getting ready to sail home to Ellsworth, and if you would like to come with me you are welcome to come aboard."

"I'd really like to come with you," I said to the Captain. "Maybe you could give me some work to do."

The Captain responded, "Well, come along with me. There will be things you can do to help me after we get under sail. I'll show you then, so don't worry."

"Thank you, I'll be happy to do whatever you ask," I said.

We arrived in Ellsworth, about sixty miles from where my father lived, quite late that evening. After we anchored the Captain said to me, "You can stay on board for the night. There is food in the cupboard if you get hungry, and there is a good bed you can sleep on. Have a good night, and I'll see you in the morning." Everyone else went ashore. I did not sleep any that night. I fastened up the cabin door, turned in, and the rats began to run. I thought there were forty horses on deck. I made up my mind that the wheel of time had stopped, and it would never come daylight. At last daylight came. I opened up the cabin door and went on deck. About an hour after the sun came up the Captain came aboard. He asked, "How did you get along last night?"

I said, "Not too bad, Captain, but I sure wasn't happy with the rats running around. It was kind of creepy, for they kept waking me up."

"Well," the Captain said, "You have already discovered one of the things a sailor has to put up with. You'll get use to them. Right now we better go into the house and get some breakfast for you."

"Before we go in Captain, I would like to know your name. My name is Charles Hanning, and I'm wondering if I earned any money on our trip up here, for I would like to have it before I go home.

The Captain said, "Charles, my name is Captain Everett Chase, and I'm hoping you will stay with my wife and me."

"Oh, I don't know about that. I'm awful homesick right now," I said.

Captain Chase said, "Let's go in the house and get some good food into you. Then we can talk about you staying and sailing with me."

We went into the house and the Captain's wife, a large noble looking woman took me right up in her arms, even though I was thirteen years old. The Captain said, "Maddie, this is Charles Hanning. Do you suppose you could fix him a good breakfast?"

"You bet I can, Everett. Charles, how about fried eggs, toast, and bacon? Does that sound good to you?" asked Mrs. Chase.

Charles was smiling when he answered, "You will never know how good it sounds to me, Mrs. Chase. Thank you."

Captain Chase said, "Maddie, Charles told me before we came in the house he wants to go home, because he's homesick."

She said, "Oh no, we want you to live with us." After she had made breakfast for me, she went to the village and bought cloth to make me some clothes. There were a couple of ladies who came to help her, and the next day I was togged out with a new suit and a boiled wool shirt on. That was something I never had before. We stayed there about three weeks, had some work done on the vessel, and loaded

Young Hanning's West Indies Ports of Call sailing with
Captain Chase and Maddie.

there with lumber for Bristol, Rhode Island. I was fitted all out with bedclothes and everything they could get for me. The Captain's wife made me promise not to leave them. Her husband was Master of a topsail schooner called the *North Branch*, and we sailed in it for two years while a new vessel was being built for him. During this time I had been to the West Indies three times.

After these trips, Captain Chase's new square-rigged brig, called *John Gillipin,* was ready to sail. She was about three hundred tons, and it was a fine vessel. Our first trip was to deliver a load of corn and wheat shocks to Matanzas, West Indies. Mrs. Chase wanted to go with us, and she was a very nice woman. When she came aboard, she had a little library with her. There were many books, and she set me right straight to studying.

When we got back to Boston there was a Captain Gilkely who came aboard. When he saw me, he knew who I was. He said to Captain Chase, "Taint that Charles Hanning? He's been missing for sometime and his mother is nearly crazy."

Captain Chase said, "Yes, that is his name, but we call him Lins."

Captain Gilkely said, "That is a nickname he goes by."

Immediately when Captain Gilkely got home to Searsport, he went to tell my folks he had found me and told Father who I was with. Father wrote my captain a sharp letter to send me home.

The captain said to me, "Why don't you sit down and write your folks a letter. Tell them the things you have told us. Tell them just how you feel. If you want to tell them they will have to come and get you, do so, for you will never go home alone. I think your parents should know exactly how you feel, Lins. Mrs. Chase will help you, because we must let them know you are all right."

I felt badly and said to Captain Chase, "I will never stay at home if I have to leave you."

The three of us talked about the best way to handle this situation. I really did not want to go home, and we decided it was best for Captain and Mrs. Chase to write the letter. I would jot off a short note as to how I felt about leaving. Mrs. Chase was very upset. She started crying when she realized that I might possibly have to go home. I could tell these two people really wanted me to stay with them, and I sure wanted to. Captain and Mrs. Chase wrote a long letter to my father stating how well I was getting along, and if he would let me stay, he would send Father one hundred dollars a year for my wages. Captain Chase also told Father he would teach me about commercial business. I'm sure my mother and father had a good long talk about letting me stay, but their final decision was a wise one. We received a letter from Father telling us that I could stay, and they were very happy that I was doing so well. Captain Chase immediately wrote a nice note to Father and sent him the money. After that the captain's wife and I corresponded with Mother, so she knew where I was. When this was cleared up, we loaded for LeHavre, France, made the trip and returned to New York. Our trips now were mostly foreign voyages, many times to Europe, and one around Cape Horn on a trading voyage.

We immediately loaded in New York with Government supplies to go to Vera Cruz, Mexico. The Captain's wife did not go with us on this trip. That was the time of the Mexican War. (This was known as the Mexican-American War of 1846-1847 and was started by the United States. It was a territorial war resulting in Mexico loosing much of its territory up north.)[3] We were laying in the bay when the city was taken. The crews of American vessels were drafted to stand guard on the stores that had been landed. (Used in this context, stores refers to the cargo carried on board.)[4] By the way, the Captain took me as Mate on that trip. I was then in my seventeenth year. When we got in the boat to go ashore the Captain felt badly. He took me by the arm, shook me, and told me, "Take care of yourself, my boy."

I asked him, "How can I do that when they will point a gun at me and shoot it off?" There were two vessel crews in the boat, and one of the Officers started to laugh, but many of the crewmembers were scared to death. When we got ashore, they dressed us up in line and called the roll. There were three Chief Officers in the crowd. They were told to step three paces to the front, and I stepped out, but the others did not.

One of the Officer's wanted to know if there were any other Chief Officers.

I told him, "There is one on the barque *E.Wilson* and one on the barque *Solutte.*

He ordered them to come out, and they came very scared.

Then a Sergeant Major came down with an order, "All of the Chief Mates are to return back aboard their vessels. We can not take the Mates out." The Sergeant Major asked me, "Where are you from?"

I told him, "I am from Ellsworth, Maine. That is where the vessel hails from."

The Sergeant Major then asked, "Are you by any chance the son of Captain John Hanning?"

I told him, "I sure am if my mother is an honest woman, and I think she is."

He said, "I know your father. When I lived in Belfast, I use to see him quite often."

He took me up to the non-commissioned Officer's dinner, and about five o'clock in the afternoon the Chief Officers were sent back aboard their vessels. The rest of the men stayed fourteen days on shore guarding the ship's stores. When they came to pay the men, they paid me the same as the rest.

Leaving Vera Cruz we sailed the Gulf of Mexico over to Havana, Cuba, where we loaded for New York. After taking a few days off, to rest and relax, we chartered for a trading cruise around Cape Horn to California. We went to Acapulco and Mazatlan, Mexico, and then on up to San Diego, California.

It was about the last of April 1848 when we left San Diego for Bombay, India, with salted hides for ballast. We celebrated my eighteenth birthday sailing the Pacific Ocean. We loaded in Bombay with cotton for Le Havre, France, and we found out about gold being discovered in California when we got there. We returned from France with a cargo to New York.

Young Hanning's European and African Ports of Call.

The Captain then got a charter to leave in ballast for Constantinople, Turkey, (former name of Istanbul,)[5] and Alexandria, Egypt, seaports on the Mediterranean Sea. There we loaded with goat's hides, matting linseed, and general cargo for New York.

Our next trip was from New York to St. Thomas, Vera Cruz, and Rio de Janeiro. Mrs. Chase wanted to go with us as it was our last sailing together. (St. Thomas is located in the U.S. Virgin Islands, approximately eleven hundred miles southeast of Miami, and just east of Puerto Rico.)[6]

After a short visit in St. Thomas we went on to Vera Cruz, Mexico. We had a nice day there and left the next morning for Rio de Janeiro, Brazil, with general cargo. Getting into Rio, Captain Chase said, "Maddie and Charles, how would you two like to spend two or three days here before we go home?"

It didn't take either one of us long to answer that question. We both said, "Yes, let's do it."

Captain Chase said, "I think this is a perfect time for us to relax and see some of the local sights."

All three of us were glad we had done this, for we not only enjoyed seeing the city, but we had time to reminisce about the years we had spent together. It also gave me a chance to tell Captain and Mrs. Chase how thankful I was for all they had done for me. After several delightful days in Rio, as the sun was setting in the west, Captain Chase said, "Time to go back to work. The fun is over my loves." We three went back to the vessel to prepare for our trip home. The next morning we loaded our holds with coffee, got the charter for traveling home, and headed for New York.

I will admit I was a bit sad knowing we were not going to be sailing together any more, but this is just a part of my life. Getting into New York, we discharged the vessel, gave each other big hugs, said our good-byes, and went on our way home.

I was with one man and his wife all this time. We had sailed together for seven years and Captain Chase worked constantly with me. He taught me about navigation and commercial business. When his wife was with us, she helped me with school subjects. Captain and Mrs. Chase took all the pains that could be taken with me in everything they taught me. They were the best people that ever lived. Captain Chase was a father to me.

I went home to see my family before getting a charter for my first sailing experience as Captain. My folks did not know me when they saw me. I had a full beard and looked several years older than I was.

GOING MASTER 1850-1855

Captain Chase was part owner of the brig we sailed in, and he wanted me to go as Master when he decided to go home. The rest of the owners thought I was too young being only twenty years old. They wanted to put an older man in, but Captain Chase said, "If you do you can buy me out, for Charles is going Master if I own in her."

The agent consulted with the owners, and they decided to get an old Captain as Mate. I would have liked my friend as Mate, but I thought I better accept their decision.

Leaving New York, I decided to wait until we got underway to tell my Mate what I expected him to do, but when I started talking to him, he turned up his nose and said, "Who's running this brig?"

I told him, "I am not going to take any of your impudence. We will discuss this later."

He replied, "I have command of this vessel and I will do as I please."

This made me mad, so I said to him, "Go to your room and stay there."

He went to his room and stayed about three days, so I took the Second Officer as Mate until he decided to quit pouting and go to work.

The old goat finally came to me and said, "I will do as you wish if you will put me back on duty."

I told him, "If you will behave yourself and do as I tell you, you may go back on duty as my Mate, but I want no more trouble with you."

We were bound for Galveston, Texas, and he did very well on the rest of the voyage until we were almost there. It was late afternoon, and I knew a storm was approaching. The sky was getting very dark, and there was a strong wind blowing to the east. I came up alongside a brig that was also going into Galveston. The Captain hailed me and wanted to know if I was going in. Before I could speak, the Mate told him, "We are not going in."

"You shut up your head," I said. Then I told the Captain, "I am going in tonight." I turned to my Mate and said, "I want you to go to your room and stay there. Do not come back out here until we are safely in. If you do, I will break you all up and throw you overboard."

The weather was bad with a really strong wind blowing, but I was able to get the bearing lights just right. I went in over both bars and up the river, let go my starboard anchor, and she swung around. Then I let go my port anchor. There were no wharves there at that time, but they had spiles. (spile: a heavy stake or timber driven into the ground as a support).[7]   I ran my hawser out on the port side after I had made fast to the spiles. (hawser: a small steel cable used to anchor a ship).[8]   I brought it in on the starboard side through the chocks, made fast, and the vessel laid there close to shore. (chocks: a block of iron with a hole in it where a rope or cable goes through to hold something securely).[9]

Shortly after we secured the vessel, my Mate came out of his room and told the Second Officer and some of the crew, "He is just a baby captain and still has diapers on." This spread through the vessel like wildfire, and the crew started calling me Baby Captain. I wondered what had happened to create this kind of talk. When the Second Officer came to tell me what my Mate had been saying about me, I started laughing. I told my Second Mate, "Now I fully understand why I'm Baby Captain. I am going to ignore this little incident, because I think they are just trying to have a little bit of fun. They are all good kids, and we've had far too much trouble on this trip. We don't need any more."

I called the Mate aft and read the riot act to him. I asked him, "What did you mean by telling my crew that I was a baby and still had diapers on?"

The old goat said, "I meant just what I said."

I said to him, "You have tried to poison my men against me, and I should have put the irons on you long ago. You have caused nothing but trouble on this trip."

He said, "I don't suppose you want me to go back with you, or do you?"

My reply was, "I sure don't. If you stay on board this vessel you will have a tin cover put over your mouth, and you will stay in the irons."

There was an awful gale blowing all night long and I was laying close to the shore. Fortunately, the vessel did not go aground. I stayed onboard the next day because it stormed so badly. When the storm abated there were eight vessels wrecked on the outer and inner bars, and three were a total loss. We had some minor damage done, so I got it fixed before leaving. The third day I hauled in and commenced to discharge. I had a nice visit with the agent before leaving, because he gave me a letter explaining how I managed to save the vessel.

The Mate packed up his things and left us. He worked his way up to New Orleans in a small schooner. He wrote an awful letter to the agent stating they would never see their vessel again, for the Captain was nothing but a baby who did not know as much as a nursing child. My Second Officer on the way down was my Mate on the way back.

By the way, the Captain of the brig that spoke to me the night before I went in was blown all to pieces. When I left, I saw he had just gotten in between two bars and was anchored. The Captain had hardly enough sail to get in with. I saw him later and he told me he thought his last day had come. He was about four weeks getting back.

I knew the owners were thinking of sending a captain down to take over the vessel, but I left before they could get one there. I was aware the New York agent would see me when I returned, and I was pleased to have the Galveston agent's letter. I did not know how the owners and agent would react with all the problems we had on this trip, but I was prepared for the worst.

When I got into New York, I wrote the agent telling him I arrived, included the bills for the work done on the vessel and the letter given me before leaving Galveston. It was several days before he came to see me, and during our visit I asked him, "Have you received a letter from the Captain I had as Mate on our voyage?"

The agent said, "A letter came from him about a week ago. It sounded like you had a pretty rough voyage."

I told him, "My Mate tried as hard as he could to have me lose the vessel."

The agent said, "Captain Hanning, I wanted to come and see you before sending another Captain down. The letter the Galveston agent gave you told the owners and me exactly how you saved our vessel. We knew you were in a bad storm, and we are grateful there was so little damage done."

I told the agent, "You certainly may put another Captain on board if you want to."

He replied, "You had better go in and fill out the papers for discharging the vessel from that trip."

I asked him, "Would you like me to charter the vessel for Captain Durham while I'm in there?"

His answer was, "You had better charter it for yourself. You are going to Galveston again, because we do not want to make a change. We are very satisfied with you as Captain of our vessel, and we all thank you for saving it from destruction. You did a good job."

Captain Charles said, "Well, I thank you for those kind words, and thanks for coming to discuss this with me. It is my wish we can put this unfortunate incident behind us. You know I had some mighty good training, and you can always count on me to do the very best I know how to do. Please thank the owners for me too."

I went in to discharge the vessel and chartered it for another trip to

Western Hemisphere Ports of Call, particularly Galveston where the "Baby Captain" saved his ship from a terrible storm while other more experienced captains were wrecked.

Galveston. There was a cargo waiting to be picked up for Boston, but before I could leave I had to get a Mate. I contacted my good friend to see if he could come and sail with me. He was the one I wanted before and a good fellow.

He said, "I'd love to, Charles. I'll be up about six o'clock tomorrow evening. I have several things to take care of in the morning before I leave. Thanks for thinking of me."

Everything went smoothly, and we had a great time on that voyage. When we got back to Boston and discharged the vessel, the agent told us there was a cargo we had to deliver to Matanzas, Cuba. After chartering the vessel and loading the cargo we were on our way. We delivered the cargo, loaded with molasses, and returned to Boston. This was one quick trip and a good one.

During the summer the owners sold the brig, and started building a barque for me, but there was a lot of work left to be done on it. I went down to help, but when they decided to sell her before it was launched, I left for Searsport. As was always the case, my family was glad to see me.

I took a room in a boarding house in Belfast not far from where my parents lived. The man of the house was a pretty wild sort of chap by the name of Bryant. They were having a revival meeting in the Methodist Church one evening, and he wanted me to go with him. Just before the meeting was closed the minister came over to me. He was a big bully minister whose name was Mr. Gillison. He asked me, "Do you have religion?"

I answered, "I always have experienced religion."

He wondered, "What does it consist of?"

I politely answered, "One must do as near right as they possibly can."

He continued to hound me. He asked, "Have you ever made an open confession?"

I was becoming a little upset with his questioning me. I didn't think it was the right thing to do in front of those attending, but I answered, "I have not made any more than living a moral life."

Then he wanted to know, "Do you think that is sufficient to save you?"

My answer, "I certainly do."

"Do you want us to pray for you?" he asked.

I said, "I have no objection to praying for me, but as I experience life I would just as well ask someone to eat for me as to pray for me."

He asked me, "Do you not believe in prayer?"

"I certainly do!" says I.

"Well," says he, "Thank God."

He went to the pulpit and raked me fore and aft. If that wasn't enough, another fellow got up and gave me a broadside.

I told them, "I did not come to church to be abused, and I consider you all to be both backwards and vagabonds. If you continue to treat me the way you have, there will be a scene right here in the church."

The minister continued his rampage, and I wasn't going to listen to it any more, so I left and went home. When Bryant came home I went to him and asked, "Did I do anything to disturb the meeting this evening?"

Quickly Bryant said, "No."

The next day when I went to dinner, one of the members of the church, who was at the meeting I attended made the expression of, "Here comes the warewoof." (werewolf: a person hiding hatred and doing little harm).[10] She was a woman that did not have the most savory character. It did not take me but a minute to open up on her. She got out of the way just as quickly as she could. This pleased the landlady where I was boarding.

Several days later, we had a very stormy day. It was sleeting and snowing, and I happened to meet the minister on the sidewalk. I went for him and was going to thrash him, but he pulled off his coat, threw it on the picket fence and said, "I am commanded to fight the devil wherever I meet him." I began to survey him. I walked around him and told him, "Go to H---." Then I walked off.

The other ministers in the city got hold of the controversy we had. I found out later that if he had gotten hold of me, he would have wiped me up in some of the snow because he was one of the most powerful men in the state of Maine. I always considered it to be about the smartest thing I ever did.

There were three that came to see me. The Baptist, Congregational, and the Universal ministers wanted to know just what had happened. I told them what went on at the meeting, and they were not very pleased with what their colleague had done.

The ministers asked, "Are you Captain Hanning's son?"

"I suppose I am," I said.

"Well," one of them said, "Your father is a Methodist minister."

I said, "Yes, he is."

These ministers went to Mr. Gillison, and he found out who my father was. I think they frightened him by telling him that if he did not apologize to me the matter would be carried in court, because it was not long after the three ministers left that he came to apologize. I told him I would accept it after being persuaded by the other minister to do so, but I had no apologizing to make to him. That settled the matter. This all took place when I was a young man.

The fall of that year the owners started building another barque, but it was going to be a long time before it was ready. They wanted me to take the topsail schooner, *North Branch*, to Havana, Cuba. We needed to get a load of molasses for Portland, Maine. By the way, when I returned the agent told me the owners sold the schooner to the old goat Captain who was my Mate on my first voyage as Captain.

During the winter, we used one of the other ships the owners had for two trips we made. Our first trip was to New Orleans loaded with bricks and hay. There we loaded with staves and went to Matanzas, Cuba, again. I took a cargo of sugar on board and made a quick stop in New Orleans where we loaded with molasses for New York.

Our second trip that winter was to the Chagres River area in Panama loaded with equipment, lumber, and supplies. (The Panama Canal Railroad, which follows the Chagres River in Panama, was started in 1850. This was of vital importance if the Panama Canal was to be built. It was not operational until 1855 and during this time several trips were made to deliver equipment. The first two years the harbor facilities had to be built. A site on Manzanillo Island was selected. Buildings, especially housing for the workers and equipment went up, and a small city called Aspinwall or Aspinville, later called Colón thrived.)[11] This was a good trip with weather and crew being almost perfect. On our way home we stopped to pick up a load of New Orleans molasses for Boston.

Returning from these trips, I went to work doing finishing touches on the vessel being built for me. About a month before she was ready, I got married. (Charles and Hannah Floyd Patterson were married on April 8, 1852, in Belfast, Waldo County, Maine). After our marriage my new vessel was launched. When I got ready to leave, my wife decided she was going with me. We had a long, rather heated discussion on this topic, and I started to think this was a very unfortunate match. My wife was bound to go with me on this trip even though I told her this vessel is not fit for a woman. She said, "I do not care, I am going with you." It was like talking to a brick wall, and I was not going to let her go on this trip.

All of a sudden a light switched on in my brain, and I said to her, "Okay, Hannah, I'll tell you what I'm going to do. Have you packed your things yet?"

"No, I have not packed my things and I am not ready to go." Hannah said.

I asked, "Hannah, how long is it going to take you?"

"I need at least two hours." Hannah replied.

"Hannah, I cannot sit around and wait for you. I have to get to the vessel and make preparations for sailing. This is what I'll do. I'll stop at the stable and order the carriage to be here in two hours, and I hope you will be ready. I'm going right now, bye."

I left and on my way to the vessel, I stopped at the stable to order the coach to pick her up in two hours. I went to the agent to charter the vessel to New Orleans, and I told him what I was going to do, why I was doing it, and gave him enough money to give to my wife, so she could meet me down south. About the time the carriage got to the house, I was several miles down the bay with a stiff breeze blowing from the northwest. I expected to see her in New Orleans. Instead I got a letter. I was scared to go home after reading it. Five months later, I sailed into New York loaded with coffee.

After discharging the vessel, one of the other agents in New York came over and told me there was a party that wanted to buy the vessel that I had been given power of attorney to sell. I had about four thousand dollars in her, and I wanted to sell her sometime ago, but no one wanted her. I had to take the time now to get rid of her before going home. I checked with the other owners to make sure it was all right with them, and to find out what their investments were, so I could figure the asking price. After the business was taken care of and we all got our money, I sent a telegram to my brother-in-law telling him; I'm coming home tomorrow and will be in about two o'clock. I'm hoping you will be able to meet me.

He was waiting for me at the steamboat wharf with his carriage when I got home.

I told him, "I hardly dare go home."

"Hey, Charles, it's going to be all right. They'll be glad to see you."

It was about two miles over to my wife's father's house where the family was waiting for us. Everyone was happy to see me, and they were glad I was home for a visit. That made me happy, for I really had not done a very nice thing to my wife the day I left.

I thought perhaps this might be a good time to take some time off and be with my family. Sitting around one day and getting bored not having anything to do, I decided to build a house in Belfast for us. We had the framing all done and were working on siding the house when I received a telegram from one of the owners of the vessels I sailed for. It read; We have been working on a very large barque for sometime and we are wondering if you would like to come up and help with the finishing work?

My reply read; Yes, I want to come. I need at least a week, because I've started building a house for my family, and I want to make sure the people helping me know exactly how I want everything done. Then I'll be up.

I told the workmen what was going on, and we went over the plans of the house to discuss finishing the interior. They continued working until the house was done, and I will say they did a very nice job. I was happy my family had a house they could call their own.

Several of the owners came down to see me shortly after I started the finishing work on the vessel. They had one big surprise for me when they said to me, "Charles, this vessel is being built for you, and we hope you will enjoy sailing in it. We are calling it *The Globe,* and she sure is a beauty."

When I got ready to go away my wife was not in a condition to go, so I had no more trouble on that account. I was gone about nine months. (This was approximately early Spring 1854.)

I left from New York with a load of lumber and equipment for the Isthmus of Panama. Leaving Panama, I followed the coastline of Central America up to about twenty-five miles south of Vera Cruz, Mexico. Black ebony, lingivity, and other native woods were being shipped to LeHarve, France, and the port of Bordeaux, a seaport in southwest France. (lingivity evidently is a beautifully mottled and curled type of Ambonia wood).[12] The consignee's wanted me to take a portion of the cargo under the main hatch for to make a port entry of it. I told them that I did not really understand how to do it. They said it was very easy, but I had to go up to Vera Cruz and see the American Counsel. He told me he would fix it and what I should do. By the way, he was a naturalized American citizen from France. I got my papers all fixed so I could sail, and we were off to France.

Arriving there, I delivered my papers to the custom house, and the men that I was consigned to all wanted the cargo at once.

I told them, "There is a little over thirteen hundred dollars in freight to pay."

They said, "We will pay the freight after it is delivered."

"I'm very sorry, but you will pay for it before it is delivered," says I.

They said, "You will have to deliver it before you can get your other cargo."

I said, "Decidedly I shall, but I will deliver it to a warehouse."

They replied, "That will do."

Then I told them, "This will be put in a government warehouse and bonded."

"That will not do," two of the men said.

"Well," said I, "I guess it will, for that is what is going to happen. If you want to pay the freight before ten o'clock you can do so, and if not I shall order the government teams down at one o'clock." They did not pay before the given hour, so I went up to the custom house and ordered the teams to be there at one o'clock. At the appointed time, the custom house officer broke the seal. My men took the hatches off and began to take out the cargo. The consignees came down with the freight money, and I told them, "You are going to have to pay the government teams I have engaged too."

They were somewhat startled and replied, "We can't do that."

They finally decided they wanted to get this over with, so payment was made. I told the stevedores to pay the teams, and I discharged the balance of my cargo without any more trouble. The ship chandler, who was an American, told me there had been a Captain Gilkely from Portland, Maine, that got about fourteen hundred dollars the same way. I loaded with general cargo while in France and returned to New York.

We quickly got a discharge and a charter to sail back to the Chagres River area in Panama with supplies. We stopped in Cardenas, Cuba, and loaded with molasses for Boston on our way home. Shortly after I returned home, my father attended a meeting of ministers at the Camp Grounds located about four miles from the house. When the meeting ended, my father and a friend came over to spend the night with us. His friend just happened to be Mr. Gillison, the same minister I had trouble with the night I went to church with Bryant. He made no reference to the previous trouble and I never saw him again.

I went up to Boston to load *The Globe* for our trip to Matanzas, Cuba. This singular instance happened when I was on this trip. I knew I was getting close to one of the salt keys of the Bahama Banks, because we were not too far from Cuba. I overtook a barque just before nightfall when we were running into foul weather. The Captain spoke to me wanting to know if I would put a lantern in my mizzenmast peak so he could follow me. (mizzenmast: the third mast or mast aft of the mainmast.)[13] I did and I shortened sail so he could keep in company. The wind was coming from the west with a good full force, and I kept on my course supposing I was far enough to the east to clear the salt keys. The weather was thick and I was further west than I had made calculations. I went below, took off my oil clothes, laid down on the bed, and heard a voice say, "Go on deck and anchor." I went up to inquire if any one had said any of the kind, and the Mate said he had not, so I went below again. Just as I got in the cabin I heard the voice say again, "Go on deck and anchor." This time it was louder than the first time. I went on deck again to investigate, and the men hadn't heard any sound like that. I went below again, and just as I got in my cabin, I heard the voice ring out loudly and sternly, "Go on deck and anchor!" I thought it was my father's voice. He was a seafaring man, but he was over thirteen hundred miles from where I was at the time. I hurried back up on deck, told the Mate to get ready to wear ship, for I was going to anchor. I told the man at the wheel to hard up, I wore ship, and let go the big anchor. The barque that was following me rounded under my stern and did the same thing. (Here are several terms to help understand what Charles was doing. Tacking is zig-zagging so as to sail either directly towards the wind or away from it. Wearing ship means to change from one tack to the other away from the wind, with the stern of the vessel turning through the wind. To harden up means to turn the wheel towards the wind so the vessel would swing around.)[14] There were considerable swells going at the time. I was drawing fifteen feet of water, and I thought I felt her take the ground.

I asked the Mate, "Do you think the vessel hit ground?"

The Mate spoke, "There was a slight tug at one point, so it is likely we did touch ground."

I told him, "Throw the lid on the port side."

He reported to me, "There are three fathoms and a half of water."

"Then throw it on the starboard side," says I.

My Mate told me, "There are nine fathoms and a half of water."

I told him, "Throw it on the port side again."

This time he reported, "It's the same as the last time, three and one half fathoms."

I told him, "Put the fore staysail and spanker on her." I put a man to the wheel and told him, "Keep the wheel east-south by east," and I laid there until daylight. I waited for it to clear up, and when the mist cleared away, I could see where I was. I found I was right on the edge of the banks of the little salt keys. They were all in sight, and I had been running for them just as straight as I could. I would have struck them in less than three quarters of an hour. The wind had sent me thirty-five miles further to the west than I had reckoned.

(The Salt Keys are known as The Bahamas Banks. There are three of them: The Great Bahama Bank, Little Bahama Bank, and Cal Sal Bank, which is the third largest and the one Charles was headed towards. It is the closest bank of the three to Cuba.)[15]

Before starting out the next morning, the Captain of the barque called to me and said, "I'll forever be grateful for your help last night. Many thanks." Both vessels survived the storm.

When I got to Matanzas, I wrote Father who was living in Searsport, Maine. I told him to write me at New Orleans, which was the next port I was going to. A letter was there for me stating all was well on the home front, so I loaded with sugar and molasses for New York. Getting in and securing the vessel, I went into the agent to discharge. He told me the owners had sold the vessel while I was gone, so I went to Searsport to see the family. I asked my father, "Did you by any chance have a dream about me while I was on this last trip?"

Before Father could answer me, Mother spoke up and said, "Yes, I heard him say to go on deck and anchor, but seeing he was an old seafaring man, I didn't take any notice of it."

Father then said, "I did dream about you. I kept seeing you running right straight for land."

"Well, Father, your message came through loud and clear! I didn't realize the wind had taken me so much farther off course than I had made calculations for, and we were right at the edge of the Cal Sal Bank. It was a close call!" My visit with the folks was a very short one this time, as I had another vessel ready and waiting to sail. All was well on the home front with everyone busy and happy, so I returned to Boston. It's always nice to check in with family once in awhile.

I thought everything would be ready for me to take off, but freights were very dull and hard to find, so I started looking for one. The ship I had now was a very large barque and carried about seven hundred tons. I went over to Blanchered and Shermans, Commission Merchants' office, on Commercial Street, to see if they had any freights, but they were having a slow period also. I decided to go outside and take a stroll around the wharf. I noticed someone standing over on the Gray's Wharf, and I trotted over for a visit. This turned out to be a good venture, because the person I met needed someone to take a cargo of ice down south.

The man asked me, "What kind of vessel do you have?"

"I have a large barque," I said.

He asked, "Would you be interested in taking a cargo of ice to either South Carolina or New Orleans?"

I asked him, "What is the freight?" He told me and I said, "If you will put a quarter of a dollar more a ton, I will take it to New Orleans."

He asked me, "How long will it take you to get your vessel into Gutord's Wharf in Charleston?"

"It will take me about an hour," I said.

He said, "Haul in there and let's go."

About one o'clock that afternoon I was taking on ice. I engaged the stevedore, but he did not stow it to suit me.

He said, "If you know more about stowing ice than I do, do it yourself."

I said, "I will do just that. Please leave my vessel."

The stevedore went uptown and sued me. He put a keeper aboard the vessel for half a day's work for his crew. I saw a lawyer and he wanted to know, "Has he presented a bill to you yet?"

I told him, "No,"

"Well," says he, "We will take care of that."

I told him, "I will be loading tomorrow."

The lawyer said, "I will see a judge and everything will be taken care of for you."

My lawyer notified this fellow's lawyer to appear the next day at ten o'clock, and I went up with my Mate. This fellow told his story, and my lawyer asked him a few questions. The Judge told the clerk to dismiss the case. I gave my lawyer two dollars and the fellow had to pay about fifteen. I took a green crew and went into the hole myself and stowed the cargo. I went out of Boston in company with a square-rigged brig.

The Captain asked me, "Are you going to keep up under the western shore?"

"No, I am going to keep out to get the wind to the east."

He said, "I am going to keep to the west for the wind will be offshore."

I told him, "Maybe we'll see you in New Orleans. Have a good trip."

That night just about dark, I saw a fog bank rising in the southwest, so I kept off as far as I could get. The wind hauled around to the south and I kept off, but about one o'clock that night the wind chopped into the northeast and it began to snow. I pointed my vessel for the south channel, and I ran out of the snowstorm. I kept along on the edge of the Gulf Stream, and I had a very pleasant passage down to New Orleans. It took eleven days and I discharged there, loaded with shocks, and general cargo for Cardenas, Cuba. On the trip over to Cuba, I met the brig at the mouth of the Mississippi River that I started out with.

Back in Boston and discharging the vessel, the agent wondered if I would be able to take a load of supplies to Changres, in the Isthmus of Panama. I checked with the owners' agent and he said, "Go for it, grab it, we are still having trouble finding freights." This was a nice trip. The weather was perfect, the crew was cooperative, everyone seemed to help each other if needed, and we all had fun on that trip. They must have known it was my last trip, for I could not have asked for a more perfect ending to four plus years as being Captain on the high seas. The owners had another vessel all ready for me, but I was going home.

I was not feeling well at all when I returned home the beginning of 1855. I also found out that I had had some heavy losses in navigation during the last year by trying to help others. This made matters even worse. When I started feeling better, I thought I would build a vessel, but gave up as my domestic affairs became unbearable. I was in a very unhappy marriage, and I couldn't handle it any longer. I did not think it was good for my girls to be in this type of environment. I sold out most everything I owned in, and settled the bills that had accumulated. It was not easy for me to leave my children, but I had to work to provide a good life for them. I told my wife, "I am done, our marriage is broken, and I am going to leave."

I went away leaving my children with their mother, and told her my agent, Mr. Prescott Ajeltine, had five hundred dollars for their care. I packed my bags and left for California about the last of August 1855. I was gone almost five years. (Charles and Hannah had two girls. Ellen had just celebrated her third birthday, and Emma was not quite one.)

CALIFORNIA, 1855-1860

It was the fall of 1855 when I arrived in California, and I went to the sea shortly after I got there. I worked in Sacramento as an officer on the Pacific Steamers that ran to Panama. These vessels carried both freight and passengers.

I was having supper one evening, and I met the Master Workman of the railroad being built between Sacramento and Folsom, California. We started talking and during our visit he asked, "Would you consider coming to work for me on the railroad?"

"Well, that sounds very interesting. I know I would enjoy it, but I cannot give you an answer right now," I said. "I'm working on the steamers and scheduled for more trips. When I finish my work with them, I'll contact you if you would like me to."

The Master Workman said, "I'm trying to get some good men on my team, so come as soon as possible. Here's how to get hold of me. On second thought, why don't you just come up when you get ready."

"Thanks, I'll be up as soon as I can," I said.

It was the first week in December 1855, and I decided to get hold of my friend from New Hampshire that lived in Sacramento. His name was Dr. Dan Morran. I went to see him and he told me, "My family and I are getting ready to trip off to Central America. I want to explore the mountains down in southern Nicaragua and northern Costa Rica. How about coming with us?"

"Gosh, that sounds like fun, Dan. How long are you going to be gone?"

"We leave on Monday and will be gone about a month," Dan said.

"Well, I have two big problems, Dan. I'm supposed to sail next week, and I have a job waiting for me on the railroad. I sure would like to go with you. I'm wondering how I can handle it."

Looking at his watch, Charles said, "I have time to go over to the Steamer's office right now and see if I can get out of sailing next week. If I can, I'll tell them I've accepted another job and I'm quitting. I'll be back in a few minutes."

I was surprised it was not difficult getting released from my job on the steamers, but they told me, "We will call you if we get in a pinch and need help."

I said to them, "I will be glad to help out anytime I can."

I hurried back to Dan's office feeling very excited about all the good things happening to me. "It's just me again, Dan, I'm back. I will go with you, but I better go and get a reservation before it gets too late. I'll be on my way. See you Monday and thanks for the invite. This will be a lot of fun."

Monday rolled around quickly and we met at the wharf before boarding the steamer. The weather was good, and we had a nice trip down the coast. We finally got to the beach area in southwest Nicaragua where Dr. Morran's family was going to stay while the two of us hiked the mountains. We were gone about ten days. We tried to keep the Isthmus of Nicaragua in sight, so we could find our way over to the Caribbean. Sitting around the campfire one evening, we started talking about how we were going to get back over the mountains to the Pacific side. Should we hike back or should we take the steamer back. We were getting low on supplies, and I must admit this was not an easy trek, and we decided to take the steamer back. The day we reached our destination on the Caribbean Sea we were very surprised when we were told the steamers did not carry passengers to the Pacific Ocean.

The only thing we could do was to start hoofing our way back up the coast to where the San Juan River entered the Caribbean Sea. We followed the Isthmus back to the Pacific side where we had left the family. We met some of the passengers we left San Francisco with, and joined Dr. Morran's family, his wife, two children, brother and sister. We stayed there three days before we got away.

(Before the Panama Canal was built the San Juan River, its beginning in Lake Nicaragua and flowing east into the Caribbean Sea, was a major navigation route that carried many people from the Atlantic to the Pacific Ocean especially during the Gold Rush Days. Even today, in 2016, there is still speculation about a canal being built so as to ease the traffic of smaller ships passing through the Panama Canal.)[16]

Sites of Hanning's Adventures in California.

There were several men there trying to make a little trouble. Their names were William Walker and Jim McNab. (Walker was desirous of personally controlling large areas of Mexico and Central America. The inhabitants would speak English, slavery would be allowed, and they would become a part of the United States. This action was known as *filibustering*.)[17]

Jim McNab was wounded in the leg in one of their confrontations and had to go back to San Francisco, and he was on the same steamer going north as we were. The Mate on the steamer from San Francisco left the vessel when they got into port and went home to New York. Dr. Morran was one of the principal owners in the company, and he got me the Second Mate's job. The Second Mate had taken the Mate's place. This McNab character had no accommodation aboard the ship. I had two bunks in my room, so I took him in with me and kept him the whole passage of fourteen days. The Asiatic cholera broke out on the ship the second day out from San Juan Del Sur. Many of the passengers were very sick and a number of them died. McNab thought there was no one like me.

When we got into San Francisco, I found out who he was. Everyone told me to be careful of him and get clear of him as quickly as I could. Then one fellow told me I was just as safe with McNab as I would be with my mother, so I let him take me around and show me the town. He would not let me spend a cent of money, and we had a jolly good time. He was full of fun. In about three weeks the steamer's office contacted me and wanted me to go from San Francisco to Panama as a Second Mate of a steamer. When I got back, I told the Pacific Steamers I was going up into the mountains to work on the railroad, and I would not be available for any more trips. I did not see any more of McNab until I went down to Marysville about three years later.

While visiting with the Master Workman of the railroad before going away he had told me, "When you get back, come on up. We'll go to work right away." He hadn't been kidding either when he said it. I didn't even have time to get settled in before we loaded up the wagon with supplies and headed to the rail site. After several days of leveling a short section of the rail-bed, we were ready to put the first sleeper down. I grabbed it up and threw it in its place and the boss said, "You can say you are the first man that ever laid a sleeper in California," and holy-smokes did we ever laugh. (The sleeper was a heavy wooden beam laid on the ground perpendicular to the tracks it supports.)[18]

I worked for the railroad until my health gave out on account of the water. I then went farther up in the mountains where I was much better. I went to prospecting with two partners and spent all the money I had. None of us had any money, so someone had to find work. I heard that Mr. Heartt wanted a barn built, and I thought I could earn some money for provisions. My friends could keep prospecting. I went to see him and started building immediately. I was finishing up the barn when one of my partners came down to see me about an area they thought would be a good investment. I told him, "I can not do it until I'm finished here. I will be done soon. Then we can go." I finished up in about a day and a half, and the owner was very happy with the barn. He paid me my money and off I went to Berry Creek.

There was a deep ravine and we went to work. Just before we knocked off for the evening, we got on a bedrock and took out a pan full of dirt. There was about forty dollars worth of gold in the pan, and we went and staked our claim for three which was nine hundred feet. We were allowed one hundred yards apiece. We notified the rest of the miners that we had struck gold there, and they all went and took up the balance of the stream. They built a dam to save our water and went down to the lower end of the claim and commenced digging. The next day we got down on the bedrock again and took out about fifty dollars. We were offered three thousand dollars for our claim, that was a thousand dollars each, but we decided not to take the offer. We went back to work the next day. After working about a hundred feet and never getting the color, we felt pretty blue. I had about fifteen dollars, and I went to the store to buy supplies. I paid that out and got about twenty-seven dollars in debt. The next day I saw something in the sluice box after the dirt had washed away. I reached in and got hold of a nugget of gold which was worth about ninety dollars. We continued panning and at the end of the day we took out about one hundred and forty dollars in all. I paid the storekeeper and we went back to work. We worked up another hundred feet, but never got the color.

I went down the mountain about fourteen miles to see if I could get a job, and I could not find anything. I bought a fifty-pound sack of flour and started back up the mountain. I got pretty tired, but I kept trudging along until I thought I was about opposite to where the boys were working. It must have been about the middle of the night when I slipped down a ravine. The sack of flour came under my head, and I went to sleep. When I woke up I was almost frozen, and it was quite some time before I could tell where I was. I straightened up, put the sack of flour on my shoulder, and staggered off down the mountain. I got down to the claim just as the boys woke up. I told them, "We have a problem. We need to get some money if we are going to continue prospecting. We are very short of food."

We continued working until we covered about half of our claim, but we were not having much luck. I said to them, "I will go and hunt up work." I went down to Bidwell Bar on the Middle Fork of the Feather River where they were building a suspension bridge. I asked the man in charge, "Do you need a good worker? I need to find work."

The man's name was Williams from Nova Scotia. He said, "No," and answered me pretty short. I went down about seven more miles to Oroville, and I could not get anything there either. I had only five dollars with me. I paid one dollar for my dinner, two dollars and fifty cents for my supper, breakfast, and lodging, which left me with only one dollar and fifty cents. When I got back to Bidwell Bar, I went into the Shade Hotel. I was sitting considering the matter. What should I do? Should I go to bed without my supper or should I pay for lodging and breakfast? I had fourteen miles to walk the next day before I could get back to the claim.

While I was thinking the matter over, Mr. Williams, the man in charge of building the bridge came in and said to one of his friends, "I have to send to Sacramento to get two bunches of four stranded rigging. The sailor that works for me told me a three stranded rope could not be spliced."

I overheard the conversation, looked up, and said, "I should like to see a three stranded rope that I could not splice."

He said to me, "How do I know you can do this for me?"

I told him, "I have pulled enough to know how."

He said, "I don't know anything about your pulling, but I will give you ten dollars if you will splice it so it will go through the block."

We went down to the Bidwell Bar Bridge they were building. I cut a thick branch of a Nancy Miller bush that is almost as hard as iron, whittled it out for a marlinspike, and I went to work. (marlinspike: a pointed iron instrument for separating strands of rope for splicing.)[19]

The sailor had cut off about half a bushel of the rope, unraveled it, and destroyed it. I put it together and spliced it in less time than it has taken me to write about it. I showed it to him, explained it to him, and told him it was stronger there than anywhere else. I put it down on a piece of board and rolled it with my foot.

He looked at it and called four or five men over. He asked them, "Can you men tell where this rope has been spliced together?"

They carefully looked at the rope and one of them said, "This is an excellent job. One would never know where it had been spliced unless we had been told."

He gave me a ten dollar gold piece and said to me, "I will give you seven dollars per day and board you, if you will take charge of the men operating the derricks so the stringers can be put in place. Williams told me, "The boss on the job, Mr. Steel, is a very disagreeable man, and the men don't like him. I will board you at my house."

I chuckled and told him, "I do not think I am in a condition to go to a private house. I have been sleeping out and there are many crawling critters on my clothes."

He said, "That's nothing. I don't believe there is a man, woman, or child in California that has not been lousy. I have a pretty wife and two of the prettiest children in California." After meeting them I think he told the truth.

I told Williams, "I want three men the first day, but before I start I have to go and tell my buddies I'm working, and I won't be mining with them any longer."

Williams said, "I'll let you do that, but you can have more men if you want when you get back."

I told him, "Three will do." I immediately started going up the river to find my friends. They were not having much luck, and they did not know what they were going to do. I told them I had found work and wouldn't be mining with them any more. I wished them both good luck and started trotting back to my job.

After a few hours sleep, I got my three men and we went to work. The men could not believe I was working right along beside them.

The boss, Mr. Steel, came up and told my workers, "I want you men to go on another job."

I told them, "Stay right where you are."

The boss bristled up to me and said, "If I want you to do something, you do it or you will have to go."

I did not say much, but I walked up to him. He began to go back, back, and he backed up against a small log, went heels-over-head, picked himself up, and started off. All the men began to laugh and holler. Steel went to find Williams to tell him, "That man you hired was going to fight me."

Williams asked, "What is this all about?"

The boss said, "I wanted the men he had."

Williams asked, "Did he let you have them?"

The boss said, "No, that is what I was going to fight him for, but if he is going to take charge you can get another man."

Williams told him, "I have got him all ready." He paid Steel off and let him go. Williams was glad he had made the change, but Steel had one man on the crew that was a very good friend. He set out to make some trouble for me.

I told him, "If you want to leave go with him."

He said, "I'm not going to." He caught up an axe and was going to strike me with it, but one of my men grabbed it out of his hands tossing him down at the same time. He picked himself up and took off, and we did not see him again. I realized the men in my crew thought everything of me. Things went along smoothly after that until the bridge was finished. Williams paid me a little over seven hundred dollars.

Mr. Williams then said, "Hanning, Mr. Heartt has a job for you if you want it. He will pay you one hundred twenty-five dollars a month. He will come to see you soon.

Several days later, Mr. Heartt came to see me, "Mr. Hanning, I would like to have you go up into the mountain to take charge of a crew of men that are working on the North Fork of the Feather River. There's sixteen hundred feet of the river that needs to be flumed. Would you be interested in the job?"

(Fluming is an artificial chute carrying water for power to move logs down the mountain.)[20]

"It sounds like an interesting thing to do. I will accept your offer," I said.

Mr. Heartt told me, "I think you really should know that the crew up there working has run off three bosses in the last month. Are you ready to accept this challenge?"

My reply, "Well, that is quite a challenge!" I started laughing, "You might just as well kill me as to send me among them border ruffians. Sure I'll do it. It sounds like a real challenge."

By the way, I had built the barn for Mr. Heartt, so I bid him goodbye, and told him to give me a decent burial when they killed me. Chuckling he said, "I'll personally see to that."

When I got up there the men were all out to work or pretending to be at work. I thought I would go to work and set up the grindstone that was laying up against the side of the cabin. When it was near twelve o'clock I got dinner, and the men came in swearing and wanted to know, "Have you come up here to boss us around?"

I told them, "I guess none of you want a boss. I did not say much more of anything to them. The next morning I got up and got breakfast. There were twelve men and I made thirteen. One of them wanted to know, "Aren't you getting up awful early?"

I told him, "I was tired of laying in bed, and I decided to get up and go to work. I tried to be quiet, and I'm sorry if I bothered you."

There was one man by the name of William Horton, who was a large Kentuckian, and an awful good fellow. He was the first to start out, and I went with him. In about an hour and a half, they all got out there to work. I worked until about eleven o'clock and called to them to get their attention. I made a motion, "My fellow men, we have enough food to have a cookout for the crowd this noon. Anyone game?"

One fellow, a Missourian, said, "I will cook if you say it is all right. I think you are the boss."

I said, "If you think I am, you may have the job of cooking." The rest seemed to be well pleased. The next morning I woke the cook up to get breakfast, and I started out a little before sunrise. Horton, the Kentuckian, followed me out and all the rest came right after us. That was all the trouble I had with them. They were all nice fellows, and they called me the Yankee Boss. I don't think there was a man out of the whole group that would not have fought for me for the least thing.

Then the boss on the river, whose name was Brise, said to me, "Take your men, go down on the river, and start grading the sixteen hundred foot claim." He put about fifty men in my gang. I divided the grading into the lower and upper section. I was in charge of only the upper one. We graded to the upper end of the claim, where we had a large bluff to blast off. I proposed to the chief boss, Brise, to go right back as far into the bluff as we wanted to, drill some deep holes, and blast it off in the deep water that was under the bluff.

He told me, "You go right in on the face of it and blast it out." It was a pretty short answer.

I told him, "Maybe you don't want me any longer."

He said, "I do not, unless you do as I tell you to."

"Well," I said, "Get my money for me just as quickly as you can."

He had about twelve miles to go down to Bidwell Bar to the office, so I took my gang, went back where I wanted to, and I put down three deep holes with churn drills. By afternoon we had them down to nineteen feet deep, twenty-one feet, and the last one was twenty-three feet. We charged them and touched them off that night. I opened up the whole length of the bluff, about fifteen inches, and the water came into the bottom the next morning. I set all the men to work cutting boughs to throw into the bottom of the seam. Then we threw clay and sand in until it was dry. I put seventy-five pounds of powder in flour sacks, put a fuse in each sack, and put them down into the holes. I put three more fuses, all of a length, and packed the seam with sand and clay that I had at hand.

I got ready to touch them off and I saw Mr. Heartt and Mr. Brise coming down the mountain. We were on opposite sides of the river from the boarding house, but we had a rope suspension bridge across the river, and they were going to come across. I beckoned to them to keep back. Everybody was running for shelter. I had three men with a live coal to touch their fuse off, and when they went off, it laid the whole bluff right over in the water for to build the flume on. Brise and Heartt came across after the bluff blew off and came up to me. Brise said, "Well, you Yankee, you did do, didn't you." I did not say any thing to him. Mr. Heartt came up and shook hands with me.

I said, "I suppose you are ready to settle with me."

"Oh, no," Mr. Heartt said.

I said, "Did you not come up to discharge me?"

"Oh, no, no," Mr. Heartt said again.

I said, "I thought Brise went down after you to come up and discharge me."

"No," he said, "That was not the intention."

I looked him in the face and told him, "I want you to tell me the truth."

He asked me, "Won't you stay and help us?"

I told him, "I will stay, but I want you to be honest with me."

He said, "We did come with the intention, but we do not want you to go."

Brise wanted to shake hands to make up. I let it all pass so I stayed. There was a bluff down about two thirds of the way where the other boss' gang was, but there was no way to blow it off down in the stream. We went down to look at it. Brise and Heartt did not hardly speak to the other boss for they were blasting right in on the face of it. They were not getting out more than a bushel basket at a time. They wanted to know what I would do there. I told them I would go right in back as far as they wanted to go, put in three holes just the same as I did up to the head, and break some away so as to loosen it up. Then we could blast in from the face and break it up into larger pieces.

They both said, "All right, you come down and do it."

The gang at that time had all gone to dinner. The boss of the gang got mad and did not go to work that afternoon. When we went in to supper, he had been drinking. He was a big stout young man. By the way, he belonged to Quincy, Massachusetts. His name was McGregory, and he was going to clean the whole boarding house out. He did a good job on all of them. I was lying in my bunk and he went for me. I jumped out of the bunk quickly, knocked his feet out from under him, and he went down on his face. I lit on his back, caught his hands, fetched them up, and I made him beg before I let him up. It was just dusk in the evening, and he started off with his Digger Indian friend who was a camp buddy. They were gone for two and a half days. We began to think he had committed suicide. The rest of the men were talking about lynching me, because I was the means of him committing suicide. The third day just before noon, he came back on the river where I was working.

He told me, "I have made a fool of myself."

I said to him, "Maybe the Almighty did it first."

He wondered, "Hanning, will you go see the main boss, Mr. Brise, and find out if he will take me back?"

"Yes, I will be glad to, but I would appreciate you not taking your anger out on people anymore," says I.

"I think I have learned a lesson. I will be a good helper," he said.

I went to ask Mr. Brise and he said, "It will be all right to tell him to go to work again, if he will work with you."

Getting back to camp, I told the worker exactly what Mr. Brise said, and everything went along smoothly until we got the flume built. We built a road down to the river at the bottom of the flume, and got all of the fluming timber out. Now it was time for me to try my luck at prospecting again.

I left this area and went up in the mountains farther to a place called Long Bar on the North Fork of the Feather River. There were five of us in company trying to get more gold out. I put in a water wheel and a pump in the river hoping it would help us get down on the bedrock, but I made a failure. Three of the men left, so that left the two of us, and we worked the surface of the river and made about twenty three hundred dollars apiece in seven weeks.

About the first of November there was a man carrying on butchering. He asked me, "Will you go in business with me?" He offered me one half of the business if I would go in partnership with him, and I accepted the offer.

One day there were two men who got on a spree. They were in liquor and they wanted one of the horses to continue on their bender. I told them, "You leave the horse alone," but they did not listen to me. I had my rifle all loaded to kill a beef, and I said to them, "You put the horse back in the stable." When they ignored me, I brought my rifle up to my shoulder. I think they got frightened and knew I meant business, because they let the horse go, and it started for the barn.

There was a large fireplace in the barroom, and there was a Digger Indian crouched in the corner close to the fire. One of them shot the poor fellow, for no cause whatever. Right away, some of his Indian friends arrested the man who shot him. They held a drumhead court martial, and he was taken out and hung in an oak tree. (A drumhead court martial is beating the membrane stretched over the open ends of a drum signaling a fight.)[21] While they were hanging him, I was killing a beef. I would not take any part in it. The other fellow sobered up and kept out of the way until the excitement was over.

By the way, one time while I was in the mountains, I had a young Digger Indian that worked for me who I called Dick. I fed him, clothed him, and he had a nice place to sleep, but the poor fellow got sick and laid down on the carpenter's bench in the back part of the house. One of the men in the butchering shop came in and said to me, "You better go out and see what has happened, for I think Dick is dead."

I went out to see what had happened and said, "He sure is dead." I had a box made, put him in it, and gave him a decent burial. Several of his Digger Indian friends were there when we buried him and they said, "Booch way no, poor Dick," booch meant good. (*Digger Indian* is a nickname given to a group of the Maidu Indian people that lived in north central California along the upper North and Middle forks of the Feather River. The name was given them by European Immigrants because they dug up roots for food. Acorns evidently were a main dietary staple along with the roots.)[22]

The owner of the butchering business had very little meat left to sell, and it was late in the fall. All of the cattle in the area had been driven down into the Sacramento Valley. We needed cattle to carry us through the winter, and two of us went down there. I bought nine steers that would weigh about seven hundred pounds apiece dressed.

It looked very much like rain when we started for the mountains, for which we had forty-five miles to go. We drove twenty-one miles the first day, then fourteen miles the next day. That was thirty-five of the forty-five, so we had ten miles farther to go, and it was snowing hard in the mountains. When we started the last day out, the farther up we got the deeper the snow was. When we got to where we turned off the Immigrant Road to go over the summit of the Mountain Road, I sent the man who went with me back with the two ponies we had. I drove the cattle as far as they would go, and I made up my mind that I had to leave them, because they began to wander off. I had about two miles farther to get over the summit. I knew when I got over the summit I could strike down on the river and get out of the snow. The snow was about three feet deep. When I started to leave the cattle, they trailed right along after me. I got down to where the snow was about eight inches deep, and I came to a place under a big fir tree. There was bare ground for about ten feet all around the tree. When the cattle saw that, they made a clip for it and laid down close to each other. I had a box of matches and a paraffin candle in my pocket. Fortunately, there was an old windfall close by, so I broke some of the limbs off and made a fire. I cut the candle in two, lit it, placed it in the limbs, and it was quite a comfortable fire. I dried myself off as well as I could, laid down with my back to the fire, and fell asleep. It was about two o'clock in the morning when I heard a voice call, "Booch." I jumped up, and the tail of my coat was all burned off. I put the fire out, laid down on the grass and dozed off for a short time. I distinctly recognized the voice that spoke to me, as the boy Dick that had died. When I woke up again, it was growing daylight. I started the cattle along the side of the mountain until I struck the trail again. I was about four miles from the Long Bar. I drove the cattle along until they could hear me on the bar, and as soon as they heard me, four or five men came to meet me. I thought I was all right until I saw them, then I collapsed, but they helped me get down to the bar when they reached me.

Three years after that, when I went to a Spiritual Circle, the boy Dick came through the medium talking Digger language. I could talk to him. He said he spoke to me when my coat was a fire. The Medium, B. F. Colson, could not speak a word of Digger language, because he had never been to California where he could see them.

It was the last part of November when I had my experience with driving the cattle in the snowstorm. I never went out again until April. I sent for a doctor about twenty-four miles away, and he charged me ninety dollars for the first visit. Before I got out, I paid twenty one hundred dollars for doctor bills. I sent a note to Sacramento to my doctor friend, who I went to Nicaragua with, and stated my case. He sent me medicine and directions that helped me feel better right away.

My partner was a very nice man about fifty-five years old. He was a Scotchman whose name was McShane. He would wait on me like a mother, but he drank an awful lot of liquor and let the business all go to the hired men. Our stack was all gone when I was able to get out. We had about four thousand dollars standing out and no money to replenish.

One fellow that worked for us, left to go home to St. Louis, Missouri. When he got aboard the steamer at San Francisco, he sent his compliments to us, telling us he had a thousand dollars of our money that we would never get. I told my friends, "I hope he dies of the Asiatic cholera before he gets home." Word was sent that he died of the yellow fever in New Orleans.

I settled up with my partner, turning over everything but one horse and saddle. I started out to go about twenty-five miles farther up the river to a place called Indian Valley. I had forty-eight dollars and the horse. I got up to a public house where I met an old friend that I had been on jury duty with in a murder case. He wanted to know, "What are you going to do up here?"

I told him, "I really do not know. I do not have much money and only a horse. I suppose I should have to sell the horse."

He said, "You stay here until I come back." He told the landlord, "Charge Hanning's bills to my account." Then he rode off with my horse. The next forenoon he came back with about seven hundred dollars he got from the miners seven miles south of Indian Valley. He told me, "You start butchering, and if you need any more money I will collect it for you."

Early that afternoon I went over across the neck of the valley where a man had a ranch. I had gotten two men to put up gallows while I was gone where I could dress cattle. I bought five steers and paid eleven cents a pound on the hoof. We judged them at a certain weight. I had been in the business before, so I could judge the weight of the cattle a great deal better than the man that I bought them from. I will say I got the better of him to about a hundred and seventy five pounds on every steer. That afternoon when I got back I killed one, dressed it, and I had no trouble selling all out that night. The next day I bought an old wagon and double harness from an immigrant that had crossed the plains who needed money. I fixed up the wagon and started peddling beef around the valley. I would go one way about twelve miles one day, then I would go another way about the same distance the next day. I did this about every third day. I was in this business seven weeks and had money enough to pay the seven hundred dollars back to my friend. This was about the last of May. I had seven head of cattle, all paid for, so I continued until Christmas.

The mining business in this area closed up, and the miners went down to the foothills. I closed up my business, crossed a range of mountains and went over to Meadow Valley where people were hoping to find gold. I started up my business again. There was one firm called Gowlinger, Thompson, and Company, that had spent about fifteen thousand dollars building a tunnel. They wanted to sink down a shaft to prospect for gold, and so far they had not even seen the color.

Before starting the tunnel, they had drilled down about ninety odd feet. They struck water so they had to go into the side of the mountain to start it. When they got the tunnel in to where they wanted to go, they sunk a shaft, but they found out the tunnel was too low, and they had to drill back up. They got in about six inches and struck water. They tried another place, got in about the same distance and struck water again. Then they drilled in as far as they dared to. They put a light charge in and touched it off. They were careful to get out of the tunnel before it went off. Water started pouring out. We were seven miles south of the prospecting area in Quincey, the County Seat, and we heard water rushing all that distance. We did not know what it was until that evening when a man came over from Rush Creek and told us what had happened. Those parties had a reservoir and a ditch that was worth about seven thousand dollars. They rigged a hydraulic hose so they could start washing down through the tunnel. Two and a half days later they got clear out to the mouth of it, but never saw the color of gold. One of them, John Gowlinger, came over to Quincey with a boy to get some supplies. A man by the name of Wilber kept a grocery store. These people owed Wilber about a thousand dollars, and he would not let them have anymore supplies. Wilber knew they owed me about six hundred dollars too. Gowlinger was about discouraged. I asked him, "What do you need, John? Make out a list of what you want." I had about a fifty pound slab of beef laying on the butcher block. I put a knife on it and looked at John.

He said, "I am not sure I will ever be able to pay you."

I told him, "It doesn't make any odds. I would not be as big a looser as you all have been." I bought beans, bacon, fifty pounds of flour, coffee and sugar, everything he wanted, and he started back with the boy and the pack mule. He had not been gone more than a half hour before the expressman came into town a hollering. We all ran out to see what the matter was.

Finally, we got him cooled down and he got out, "Gowlinger, Thompson, and Company, are the richest men there are in California. They cleaned up a hundred thousand dollars this morning." Everybody got on their horses or mules and started over to where they were. When we got there, the gold was in the pan and the pan was almost full. There was a little over twenty three thousand dollars when they weighed it. When they got down to the mouth of the claim, where the rivets were in the sluice boxes, they began to see lots more gold. That was after Gowlinger had left to come to Quincey. He did not know anything about it until they got back to camp. That was about the middle of June 1858, and by the Fourth of July they had cleaned up over one hundred and seventy thousand dollars. Someone offered them a million dollars for it, but they did not take it.

A day later, John Gowlinger came to me to say, "Thank you, Mr. Hanning, for what you did for us. I'm here to take care of our debts."

I had about four hundred dollars in bills, and I told him, "I would be happy if you would just pay my bills." The firm talked the matter over. They paid all of my bills, and gave me the money for the provisions I gave to them. My health got poor again, and I settled up and started for San Francisco.

I got down to Marysville and the State Fair was going to be there the next week. I could not get a room anywhere. Then I saw Jim McNab again, who was now in Marysville trying to make his living by gambling. He is the guy who was wounded in Nicaragua, and he was known to be one of the worst desperadoes there was in California. He told me, "The rooms are all taken up, so you will be staying with me while you are here. If you have any money with you, I want you to put it into the hotel safe."

I told him, "But I want some money to pay my bills."

He said, "Your bills will get paid, and you do as I tell you."

The clerk told me, "It will be a good idea to put your money in the safe. You really don't have to pay for anything while you are here in the hotel, for we will give you a bill before you leave." Afterwards the clerk told me, "Be careful not to get in any trouble with anybody while you are here, for Jim will shoot them in a minute if anyone insults you."

After I had located my room with my friend McNab, I went around to see some of my friends, acquaintances, and the Mayor, who had two partners. The Mayor's name was Height and his partner's names were Decker and Smith. They told me they were building a bridge across the Yuba River. Smith said to me, "We sure can use more good help. Any chance you would like a job while you are here?"

I asked him, "What will you pay me?"

He said, "I'll pay you seven dollars a day."

"I'm always ready to go to work. When do you want me to start?" I said.

I reported that afternoon, but when I got on the job I found that Steel was the boss. He did not know me at first, and he gave me a gang of men on a portion of the bridge. The next forenoon he discovered that I was the man that had superseded him on the other bridge. He took me off and put me in the gang carrying heavy planks across a difficult place. I told him, "You should go to where they do not rake up fire overnight."

I had worked three quarters of a day, and I went to the office to get my money. Just as I was going out the door, I met the mayor, his two partners, and Judge Eva. The Judge took me by the shoulder, shook my hand, and said to the men, "This is one of nature's honest men. He has left the mountains without owing a dollar."

The Judge gave me an introduction to his friends. Smith said, "We know Mr. Hanning, he has been working on the bridge for us."

"Well," says the Judge, "He is a mechanic, every inch of him, and a capable man."

Mr. Smith said, "We all want you to go back on the bridge again."

I told him about my trouble with Steel at Bidwell Bar. "I will not work under him."

Smith said, "I will give you a gang of men if you will go back to work for us. You won't have anything to do with Steel," so I went back. Smith took about seventy-five men out of Steel's gang of only about one hundred and twenty five men. He told Steel that he wanted me to take them to the other end of the bridge.

"You can take the whole gang if you are going to do that," Steel said.

Smith said, "All right, Mr. Hanning, I want you to take charge of the whole gang."

Says I, "All right."

Steel left and I went on trying to get part of the bridge finished so it could be used. We worked on one side, for in two days they were looking for the first arrival of the folks to come to the State Fair. We made pretty good progress the first day. When we quit work that evening, I said to my men, "You all get as many men as you can find tonight to come to work tomorrow morning." I must say, we had a fine group of men working the second day. Nightfall came all too quickly. We were not quite finished with the one side, and I asked the men if they would work all night. They all readily agreed, and the next morning we had one side of the bridge done so people could cross. Just as we laid the last plank down on the finished side there was a team on the other end of the bridge, and people began to pour in.

Smith and Decker came down about 8 o'clock in the morning when they saw the teams coming. They came up, caught me by the hand, congratulated me with doing so well, and said, "We sure made a good change."

At about 11 o'clock Judge Eva came down with all three of the men to tell me, "At noon the hotel will have dinner all ready waiting for us." My men and I worked for an hour and went up to the Shade Hotel to have a good dinner. There I met my friend McNab. I told the men, in a brief interview, the circumstances of how I came to get acquainted with him and what he had done for me. When I introduced him, he behaved like a gentleman. The Mayor and his party knew about him, but they told me to invite him to dinner. After dinner he excused himself and went off, but told me before he went, "I do not want to stay with your company. They are too respectful for me."

I laughed and told him, "All right."

The next day we went back to work on the other side of the bridge, and we made good progress. The Fair commenced the next day, and we knocked off for two days. Then we finished up the bridge. The first day of the Fair I saw Steel coming out of a drug store with his head all tied up. Some of the boys had got aboard him, and beat him up pretty badly. After the bridge was all finished, I continued my journey to San Francisco.

I was not very well at the time, and I went to see a Dr. Cooper. He examined me and wanted to know, "Do you have a thousand dollars?"

I told him, "It doesn't make any odds to you so long as I pay my bills."

"Well," he said, "If you had, I could keep you here and get every dollar of it, but here is a prescription you can get for five dollars. It will do you as much good as for a thousand."

Looking at him I said, "I guess I picked a quack doctor."

He replied, "I think it would do you good to take a trip across the Pacific Ocean."

I wasn't quite sure just how I should take this remark. Did he feel this would be good for me, or was it because I called him a quack doctor and he didn't like it? It made no difference to me for I thought it was really a good idea.

I went to look for a vessel to get a passage to China, but there was but one vessel going there. The Captain wanted a Second Mate. He would not take a passenger, so I made a bargain with him and went aboard the barque for Hong Kong, China. I don't remember the date but it was sometime in July 1858.

Our cargo was both dead and alive Chinamen, about four hundred in all and half of them were ashes of dead bodies. Everything went smoothly, but we could not get a freight in Hong Kong. We went down through the Philippine Islands to Batavia, a city on a Dutch Island in the archipelago called Java. We had hopes of getting a cargo for San Francisco, but we found nothing there either. (Batavia is the former name of Jakarta, located on the northeast corner of Java Island.)[23] The Captain was not making any money on this trip as business was very dull. In fact he was losing it, so he was quite bilious and disagreeable. The two of us had a little conflict about this situation, and I had no more trouble with him until we got to sea, but he was very abusive to his Mate. The Mate was a nice man, but he had no backbone and he stood the Captain's abuse. I told the Mate, "If he ever gets aboard me he will get all that belongs to him."

In our passage back to San Francisco we carried away our main topmast. It was just at daylight in the morning. We cleared up the wreck as we had a spare topmast on deck. When they were ready to send it up, I asked the Mate, "Are you not going to send down the main yard first?"

He did not give me any answer. They got the topmast started, just got it into the cap, but could not get it any farther.

I stood looking on, and the Captain told me, "Help us heave on the capstan."

I told him, "It's no use, we have to send down the main yard first." I told him flatly, "I will not help heave on the capstan."

He spoke loudly and said, "This ship is in a state of mutiny." He went to get his revolver.

I went to my room to get mine. When I got back out he wanted to know what I had the revolver for. I told him, "You said this ship was in a state of mutiny, and I decided the first man that showed any signs of it would have seven holes through him."

The Captain turned white, trembling like a leaf. He told me, "Go to your room and stay there."

Says I, "All right."

He quickly changed his mind and told me, "Get to work and send this topmast up."

I told him, "Any D--- fool ought to know it will not go up without the main yard being unshipped and the truss band swung around." I said, "If you will let me have my way, I will do it."

He said, "Go ahead."

I took charge, hauled the topmast back down, lowered it on deck, unshipped the main yard, swung the truss around, sent the topmast back up, got the head of it through the cap on the main mast, and sent the topmast rigging up. Then I sent the main topmast home, put the fid in the heal, shipped the main yard again, reaved up my topmast rigging, sent the tatagla royal mast up, put the rigging on, and set it up temporarily. (Tatagla is the name of a hardwood tree, found in the Philippine Islands.)[24] I sent my top lanyards up, bent the sail, and had upper and lower topsails on.

About half past nine I turned in as I was pretty tired. My watch was at twelve o'clock. I didn't wake up until seven bells the next morning. I asked the Mate, "Did you call me for my watch last night?"

He said, "No, the Captain ordered me not to."

I told him, "I do not care anything about what the Captain said. When it is my watch on deck, I want to be called."

The Captain evidently heard what I said. When he went to breakfast, he told his Mate, "This Second Mate Hanning is the second Californian I have had for an officer, and both times I have felt that my life was in jeopardy. I have felt that way all the time on this trip ever since we left Batavia." He told his Mate, "I am sure he would have shot me yesterday in a minute, if I had offered to raise my revolver."

The Mate told the Captain, "I am very sure he would have done so."

The Captain told his Mate, "When I get into San Francisco, if I ever do alive, I think I will let him go."

We got along smoothly all the rest of the voyage. When we got in to San Francisco he told me he did not want me any longer, but he wanted to know if I would stay and discharge the vessel. About the time we got discharged there was a Boston vessel that came in, and I saw by the paper that it was the

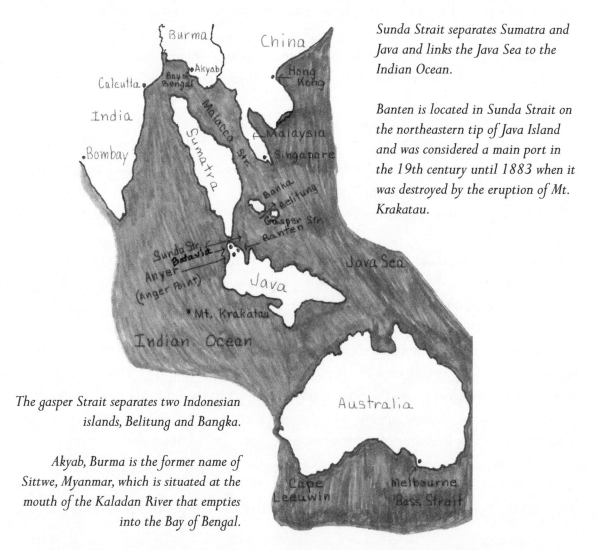

Sunda Strait separates Sumatra and Java and links the Java Sea to the Indian Ocean.

Banten is located in Sunda Strait on the northeastern tip of Java Island and was considered a main port in the 19th century until 1883 when it was destroyed by the eruption of Mt. Krakatau.

The gasper Strait separates two Indonesian islands, Belitung and Bangka.

Akyab, Burma is the former name of Sittwe, Myanmar, which is situated at the mouth of the Kaladan River that empties into the Bay of Bengal.

ship *Lucknow* under Captain Gorman. He and I were acquainted. He was a particular friend of mine, and I went to see him.

Captain Gorman wanted to know, "Do you have a vessel here?"

I told him, "No."

Captain Gorman said, "I have discharged my Mate and I want you to go with me." I packed up my things for the next trip.

Then I went to the old storm bird Captain Robinson, and told him I wanted to settle up with him. He told me, "I thought you would be going on the next trip with me."

I told him, "I have a friend that just came into port, and he wants me to go with him."

He paid me my wages and told me, "I hope you have a safe trip."

I shipped as Mate on the *Lucknow*, the very last of December 1858 to Melbourne, Australia. We had a fine passage from land to land in about forty-seven days. It took ten more days to get into the Straits of Bass before going into Melbourne. From there we went around Cape Leeuwin, up to the Province of Banten, located at the northern tip of Java Island. (I believe the area Charles referred to as Anger Point includes the cities of Anyer, Batavia, and Banten.) We sailed the Sunda Strait into the Straits of Gasper. Leaving this area, we went north to Singapore, and through the Straits of Milacca, sailing up to Akyab, Burma. When we got into Akyab we had orders to go to Calcutta, India.

They started loading our vessel about a week after we arrived, and it took them two months to finish. We hauled out in the stream and there came up a terrific wind. We collided with two other vessels cutting our minniamast spring down, and we hauled back into moorings and laid a month longer. We finally left Calcutta and headed to Boston. This would take us about one hundred twenty-four days.

This was a long trip, but while we were in Calcutta, I fell in with one of the most remarkable men I ever saw. He was a Buddhist Priest of Persia. He knew the most of any man I ever talked with. He told me more about the United States than I knew myself. I learned more in the two months that I was acquainted with him than in all my previous life. He told me of the planets, the different religions, how the city was built, and about the nations of the world. He said the Americans were the brightest people, because they were the most western nation on the earth. He would come aboard the ship every day but Sunday to take dinner with me. We would talk about everything. He could talk seven different languages. While visiting in English, he could speak the language just as fluently as I could and as plain. He told me, "You do not know what *poor folks* are, because the Americans have everything to make them happy." We had a good government, but we held slaves. That was not right, but it would be overcome by greater minds and then the slaves would be free. He told me the Americans were prosperous, that we had large hearts with a Christian spirit, and were always ready to respond to those who were in need. He told me about my nationality from birth and my past life. He told me the minute and the hour that I was born. I liked the man. I would like to have seen him again, but that was fifty-one years ago. He was quite an old man then. We got into Boston about the middle of January 1860 with our crew all frostbitten. Nine men went to the hospital frozen.

Leaving Boston, I immediately went to Belfast, Maine, where my children were and took them from their mother to take care of them. I commenced proceedings for a divorce from my first wife, Hannah Floyd Patterson. After getting the girls settled with my dear friends, who lived in the country a short distance from town, I no longer worried about them for I knew they were well taken care of. Incidentally, the man of the family was a captain himself, and later became my brother-in-law. Captain Russ wanted me to take his barque, *Laura Russ*, to Matanzas, Cuba. When I returned to New York, he wanted me to go to Liverpool, England, but my lawyer said, "You better not go until after the May court. I might need you during the day of the trial."

I was more or less in limbo having to wait around for the court system to declare our marriage dissolved, and my old agent asked me to take charge of helping build a brig for one of his Captains. I enjoyed that. When the brig was finished, Captain Russ wanted me to to take his vessel to Cardines, Cuba. I rather liked these short trips, and I went and had a good time. (Hannah and Charles' divorce was finalized May 1860.)

During the latter part of the year 1860, everyone was talking about the possibility of a Civil War breaking out between the North and the South. I knew right away what I eventually would have to do if this happened.

This is another instance in my life when I was following the sea. A particular friend of mine asked me to go as Mate to the West Indies with him. I told him, "If I go with you it will break up our friendship."

He wanted to know, "Why will it do that?"

I told him, "Because you have never had a Mate that suited you."

"Well," he said, "You would," so I shipped with him.

As soon as we left the wharf, I went forward to clearing up, and I was starting to cockbill the anchors so they would be all ready to let go if need be. It was what all vessels do until they get out to sea. My friend, the Captain, came forward and began to give orders. I went aft, but when he discovered that I had gone, he came aft and wanted to know, "Why are you not attending to your duty?"

I told him, "I shipped out to take charge of one end of the vessel, and if you want the forward end, I will take the aft."

We read the riot act over to each other and he said, "This is mutiny."

I told the man at the wheel, "Put the wheel up and let her whirr around. Take me back to the wharf."

The Captain ordered the man to keep her on her course. After we had a loud talk, he told me, "If you will take the forward end, I will keep the aft."

I told him, "All right." I never went with a better man than he was, but he kept his place, and I kept mine.

When we were in Cardines, the men wanted liberty to go ashore. The Captain said, "That would not do. They would leave."

I told him, "I will be responsible for the men."

"Well," he said, "Then they might go."

I told him, "They want five dollars apiece."

"Oh no," said the Captain.

I told him, "Captain, I will let them have the money if you do not have it."

He said, "I will let them have the money, but you know what they will spend it on!"

I told the men before they left the vessel, "If you go ashore and get drunk, do not come back aboard until you get sober."

The next morning they were all back, ready to go to work except one. About three o'clock in the afternoon, the missing man came down to the shore and hailed the vessel. I sent the Second Mate, with two men ashore to pick him up. When he came aboard he was so drunk he could hardly stand, but he backed up against the rail and said he was ready to go to work. I told him, "You had better go to the forecastle and go to sleep. I will call you when I want you." I did not see anything more of him until the next morning.

The Captain's wife went ashore on Sunday morning, but the Captain did not go until later in the day. Shortly after he left, I left the vessel in charge of the Second Officer and went ashore. I was sitting down at a table on a second floor veranda with some Mates talking with them. My Captain was in a similar place right across the street visiting with other Captains. Our crew and a lot of other sailors got to fighting in the street right underneath us. My Captain spoke across the street and said, "Mr. Hanning, our men are fighting down there."

I said to him, "Let them fight."

The Captains decided to all go down to the street, thinking they could break up the fight, but in the process several of the Captains got hurt. My Captain got his lip cut, and one of the other Captains got his arm broken. This all happened while I sat calmly looking on.

When we got back to Boston, the Captain was asked by one of the agents, "How did you get along with Mr. Hanning?"

He said, "First rate, I never had a better man."

Then they asked me, "How did you get along with the Captain?"

I told them, "All right."

They said, "You had trouble with him before you got out of the harbor, didn't you."

I told them, "Yes, but that was all the trouble I had while I was with him."

At this point of my life all I wanted to do was go home and be with my children and best gal for a while.

AMERICAN CIVIL WAR YEARS 1861 - 1864

I was fortunate to be able to stay at home for a few months with my children, and when the Civil War really started, I knew I had to enlist. On April 29, l861, I enlisted as Elisha Hanning in the volunteer Army, Company K, Fourth Infantry Regiment of Maine, to serve for three years. Men from all over the state of Maine reported to Rockland and we headed for Washington on June 17. They gave us our muskets, a small amount of training, and sent us off to war. I fought in every fight that our company fought in, except Gettysburg, from the First Bull Run (July 21-August 29,1861) up through the second day in the Wilderness Battle (May 5, 1864).

During our first year of the war in 1861, we saw very little fighting. The one fight we had was the First Battle of Bull Run and it was a whopper. We all got a good taste of what we were headed for, as we lost a number of men and many were wounded.

When the year rolled over into the beginning of 1862, we were into

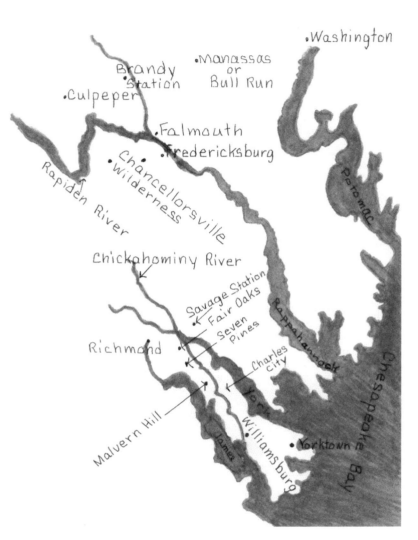

Civil War battles Charles Hanning fought in, including the battle of The Wilderness where he was wounded.

a full-blown war with the Confederate Army. During April and May we were in Yorktown right smack in the middle of the Siege. Immediately after that, we headed to Williamsburg for our second fight of the year. The end of May we were ordered to fight in the Seven Pines and Fair Oaks Battle. This battle included the Chickahominy River area and Charles City crossroads. On June 29 we fought at Savage Station where we lost quite a few men.

Immediately we went on to White Oak Bridge and Swamp and Malvern Hill where we had skirmishes that produced some serious fighting on July 27 to 30. During this early stage of the war if there was a lull in our fighting, we were all very quiet. It's a grueling task killing people day after day and very often thinking, will I be next? These were our thoughts during most of June and July. The Second Bull Run fight was August 27 throughout the rest of the month. We did have several minor fights during September, but nothing that amounted to very much. December 12, 1862, was the First Fredericksburg battle. All of the fighting we did this year was in the state of Virginia.

1863 arrived, but I was unable to fight in any battles until I returned to my regiment about the middle of April. The beginning of May we had a four-day fight going on at Chancellorsville. Then I was out of commission until early fall. On October 13 our regiment fought at Bristoe Station, which included the surrounding area of Kelly's Ford, Brandy Station, and Rappahannock Station.

Our first and the only battle I fought in 1864 was the Wilderness Battle. This is a thumbnail sketch of my life during the Civil War.

During the winter of 1861, we were at camp in Alexandria, Virginia. There were cards, poker games, and many board games given us, but we got bored playing these simple games, and if someone thought of something to do we got involved.

This was one of those events. One of the men in our company wanted to challenge the men in the regiment to wrestle him with a back hold. One man jumped at the chance. He tried three times to throw the wrestler with no success. The wrestler wanted him to try once more, but he had had enough. "Please, no more. I give up. You are a lot stronger than you look." Everyone watching started to chuckle.

The challenger said, "I admire your courage, but you are a fool for there is not a man in the regiment that can throw me."

I Sergeant Hanning spoke up, "I'll wrestle with you."

The wrestler said, "Do you really want to take me up on it?"

"I'm ready whenever you are. Just tell me," says I.

The wrestler replied, "Hanning, I'm always ready, but I don't think you are."

Hanning said, "I sure am," and all of a sudden down the challenger went on his back. I told him, "We can try again if you want to." When we got ready, he came down with such a force I landed on top of him. It took two of the men to help him get up. With a smirk on my face I asked him, "Are you satisfied or do you want more?"

The wrestler said, "No, I sure don't. Holy gee what a powerhouse. No one has ever done that to me before."

I told him, "There are men in this regiment that could hold me out to arms length, and I could not help myself."

Another instance that happened shortly after the wrestling match, got the Colonel's attention. There were two really nice men that got very drunk. They were Sergeant Libby and Private Velmer. They went to the Colonel for an order to get more liquor, but he would not give it to them. He told them, "Go to your quarters, sleep it off, and you'll feel a lot better." However, they were in a fighting mood and went after the Colonel. The Colonel ordered them arrested. He sent his aide to the officer in the guard tent telling him to find these two men and put them under guard. The officer sent a Corporal and two Privates to get them, but Libby and Velmer picked on the Corporal and cleaned him out. The Privates ran to the Colonel to tell him what had happened.

The Colonel came to me. I was sitting in my tent writing a letter. The Colonel came in and said, "Hanning, will you go see if you can find Private Velmer and Sergeant Libby? They are roaming around out there drunk, and the men from the guard could not handle them. I am not asking this of you as an order but as a favor, because they need to be arrested."

I was not on duty, and I hesitated for a moment, but quickly I said, "Yes, Colonel, I'll get ready."

"Thanks Hanning. I knew I could count on you," and the Colonel left.

I got up, put on my side arms, went down to the guard tent, and got two Privates. We marched up to the Colonel's quarters to tell him we were ready.

The Colonel said, "Take them dead or alive. If they show any resistance shoot them right down."

When I went after them, they were out on the parade ground smashing their fists together saying what they were going to do. When they saw me coming, Sergeant Libby slunk backwards going towards his tent. Velmer stood up straight as a candle. I said to the Privates, "You two go after Velmer. It doesn't look like he is going to be too difficult to control. Just make sure he doesn't get away, and walk him to the guard tent. If he resists, shoot him down. I'll get Libby under control."

I walked slowly towards Libby saying, "Halt! Libby, halt! I will shoot you down."

Looking sheepishly at me, he stopped and slowly walked back towards me. I locked him in my arm as we walked off to the guard tent.

When we got there Sergeant Libby said in his slurred voice, "Put us in on the right. It's more quiet over there." A place was made up for them to sleep, and I went to my quarters.

Early the next morning the Colonel went to the guard tent and told Libby and Velmer, "Go to your quarters and I will see you later." After Guard Mounting he sent for them, gave them a regular reprimanding and told them, "If you ever do anything like that again, you will be punished." He sent them back to their quarters, but after they started out, he called them back and asked them, "Why did you resist Sergeant Hanning?"

Libby puckered up his mouth, half laughing and said, "I saw kill in Hanning's eyes, but I didn't in the first men you sent."

During the war I was wounded twice. The first time was at the First Battle of Fredericksburg (December 11-15, 1862). I had my right shoulder dislocated, and I was taken prisoner. I will say the

Confederates did everything that could be done for me, and they did a good job. They carried me to Libby Prison in Richmond, Virginia. (His shoulder was most likely set in a field hospital, a short distance behind the lines, before he was carried to the prison.) When I was released from prison the Union sent me to *Camp Parole* in Annapolis, Maryland, where I stayed for several months. (Handling the prisoners was a problem for both sides of the war. If they wanted to be released they had to swear they would not take up arms against their captors until an exchange was made.)[29]

After my prison experience and waiting in Camp Parole to be exchanged, I went back to my regiment at Falmouth, Virginia. Shortly after I returned, the Union Army moved to the Second Fredericksburg Battle (May 3, 1863). Our division was engaged at Chancellorsville (April 30 to May 6, 1863). The third day our army fell back across the Rappahannock River, and we went in the old quarters of the Union Army. I was not feeling well at all, and they sent me to a hospital in Washington where I was told I had typhoid fever. I was really sick for a good two months. I'm sure I caught the fever while in prison, because the place was full of sick men and it was very dirty. After I started feeling better, they sent me to Fort Schuyler on Long Island Sound, New York, to the convalescent hospital. Incidentally, while I was there, my nurse was the sister of Mr. Gillison, the bullying minister from Belfast. I was released from the hospital on July 3, 1863, and given a furlough of thirty days to see and look after my two girls, ten year old Ellen and Emma eight years of age.

While I was in the hospital, the Army under General Hooker moved on to Gettysburg (July 1, 1863) where it had three days of fierce fighting. I felt badly I could not be with our team, but I was told our troops did a super job, and it was a victory for the Union.

When my furlough was up, I went back to Fort Schuyler to be released. About the middle of August, I joined my regiment which was laying at Sulphur Springs, Virginia. Sulphur Springs is a very small village near the Rapidan River and in the vicinity of Culpeper, Virginia. (The cavalry unit of the Union Army of the Potomac and the Confederate Army fought at the Battle of Culpeper Court House on September 13, 1863. This resulted in a Union victory. General Meade sensed General Lee's movement in his lines and pushed the troops in the Army of the Potomac to the Rapidan River.)[30]

There was severe fighting in this entire area throughout the war, and this was the beginning of many skirmishes

Emma and Ellen Hanning in the period oval frame that Charles Hanning took with him on his various vessels and other travels.

I fought in after my return to my regiment, including Brandy Station, Kelly's Ford, Bristoe Station, Rappahannock Station, and the Battle of Wilderness, May 4-6, 1864. The Union troops were trying to securely hold the ground for the Union.

Sometime during late November, we had another fight at Brandy Station where we drove the Rebels out of their winter quarters. The Army of the Potomac laid there all winter with the exception of our corps that were out surveying the surrounding area seeking information about the enemy.

These are some of the unhappy instances that happened while I was in the Army. It seemed as though our winter breaks almost always lead to problems with the men, for they did not have enough to do to keep them occupied. After we got settled down for winter, the inspecting officer inspected our brigade. He said, "You are the dirtiest regiment in the Army of the Potomac. There is only one man that is fit to go on inspection and that is Sergeant Hanning of Company K."

The Orderly Sergeant of our company was Sergeant James E. Doak. There was a lot of talk going on that Doak might be promoted to Second Lieutenant. However, there were not enough men in our platoon to warrant his promotion, so he was ordered to remain in his position as Orderly Sergeant. He did not want to do it, because he expected to get mustered out of the service. During this time, Sergeant Sears Nickerson was acting Orderly.

Then an order came through to me. It read; *Sergeant Hanning, you are being ordered to fill the position of Orderly Sergeant of your squad.*

I went and told the officers, "I will not do it without an orderly's warrant."

Then the Colonel came to me and said, "Hanning, you have to take the Company."

I looked at him and said, "Colonel, I will take this position as soon as I have an orderly's warrant."

The Colonel replied, "If you do not take it, I will put you in the ranks."

I said, "Go ahead."

Then General Ward told Captain Nash, "Go get the paperwork needed for an orderly's warrant, fill out the information on it, and get it to Hanning as quickly as you can. Hanning has told the Colonel he will take the position as soon as he gets the warrant."

The next day we went on brigade drill in the afternoon. When I went back into my tent I found a large envelope on my bed. I opened it and there was the warrant.

When Sergeant Nickerson found out about this he was really mad. The reveille beat for dress parade the next morning, and I went out and ordered our squad to fall-in, but they did not obey the order. I spoke sharply and they started to take their place.

Sergeant Nickerson said, "What's going on?"

I told him to take his place in the rear of the Company, but he kept rattling on. Again, I told him to take his place or I would have to put him under arrest. He finally obeyed.

The dress parade went on as usual, and when the Orderlies were called to the center, I told the

Adjutant, "I have no report to make, Sir."

The Adjutant replied, "That's all right, Sergeant Hanning."

The next morning at roll call, Sergeant Nickerson again wanted to know what all this meant. I told him, "Go see Captain Nash. He will tell you what is going on."

Now that the Orderly situation had been taken care of, I had to face the men about cleaning up our company. I went to the Captain to ask for two days to clean everything up. The Adjutant reported in about half an hour that I could have it. He also said, "You can even have more time if you feel you need it."

I went right to work making preparations for soap, water, large camp kettles, and rags. Then I got the men ready for cleaning up. I had them all working. Even our company grounds were getting polished. The biggest problem was getting them to clean themselves up.

I talked with Captain Nash, General Ward's aide, as to what I should do with Sergeant James Doak. I said to Captain Nash, "He is not helping us with cleaning things up."

Captain Nash said to me, "He had his choice to either take the Company or go back to Fourth Sergeant. He told me he wanted to go back."

"Well, he is still acting like a Lieutenant," says I.

Captain Nash said, "Trot him out like all the rest and have him clean up, for he is as dirty as anyone else."

I sent a Corporal to see Doak to tell him to come out and help clean up. Doak sent this message back, "Tell Orderly Hanning to go to H---."

I stepped over to headquarters and reported to Captain Nash what Doak said.

Nash said almost the same thing he said before, "Trot him out like all the rest and have him clean up. He is just as dirty as the rest of the crew."

I went to see the Officer at the guard tent and said, "Sergeant Doak is refusing orders to come and help clean up our company. I want you to send a Corporal and two Privates to get Doak up here even if the men have to drag him all the way, because I'm responsible for him."

One of the Privates came back and told me, "Doak gave us quite a struggle. We tried to explain to him what was going to happen if he didn't come with us, but even that didn't work. We had to use brute force to get him to the guards and he is really mad."

I guess Captain Nash did not feel I was handling this properly, because he came over to my tent. He was furious and not talking very nicely to me.

I said to him, "Captain, I have no jurisdiction over you, but I will report you for talking to me that way."

Captain Nash quickly left saying, "I am going to your friend Captain Libby to tell him the circumstances. The adjutant happened to be present and they both said, "Nash, you go back to Hanning and apologize. This is rediculous."

Then the Adjutant said, "You can't do this too quickly."

Captain Nash did come to apologize. Then he went to the guard tent and told Doak, "You have to go help with the clean up, and you must clean yourself up. If you don't do it, you will stay right here under guard and be court-marshalled for disobeying your superiors."

Doak said, "I will go and help with the clean up if Hanning will call the guard away."

Word was sent to me that Doak was going to do as I asked, if he could get out from under the guard. I wanted to make sure that it was within my jurisdiction to release him. I was advised to discuss this with General Ward. While visiting with him, I begged for Doak's mercy. General Ward went over to the guard tent with me, reprimanded Doak and told him to go clean up. About every officer in the regiment came to my tent to say how happy they were.

Saturday afternoon when we went on inspection, Captain Nash told the crew, "I'm happy to report today that the Fourth Maine Regiment is the cleanest regiment in the brigade, with the exception of one man. That man is Sergeant Nickerson."

I talked to Sergeant Nickerson saying, "You must clean yourself up and be ready for an inspection Sunday morning. Then we can all be really proud of ourselves, Sergeant."

He was ready and I did not have any more trouble with him or any of the other men.

There came a very rainy day when five of our men went out and got liquor somewhere. They became very noisy, laughing, and yelling. Captain Nash went out trying to stop them, but they were going to lick him, and he came into my quarters. He began to use language unbecoming of a Captain.

I asked him, "Captain Nash, do you see the corner hole I cut into my cabin? Get out through it as quickly as you can."

On the outside of the hole, there was a log about six inches through (diameter) that he had to step over, but he slipped and fell down on his back in the gutter where there were about four inches of dirty, muddy water running. He had to roll over to get up, and he was covered with mud.

Captain Nash immediately went to the Adjutant to report what I had made him do, because he wanted me arrested. The Adjutant told Nash he would do it. My friend Captain Libby was in the Office. The Adjutant said, "You better not be too fast before you start a case against Sergeant Hanning. He is a good honest man and if he feels it is the right thing to do he will stand up to you or anyone in his command. You might get yourself into trouble." That had the effect of bringing Captain Nash to his senses.

Captain Libby asked Nash, "What is the cause of the trouble?"

Nash said, "I went to Hanning to order him to take care of the men, because the liquor they were drinking made them looney. They were a whooping and hollering having a grand old time, and I felt they must be stopped."

Libby then asked, "How did you approach him?"

Captain Nash replied, "Well, I suppose I did speak a little kind of rough."

Captain Libby said, "Now we are coming at it. What did you say to him?"

Nash paused, then answered, "I asked Hanning what kind of a D_ _ _ orderly are you?" That's when he wondered if I saw the hole he had made in his quarters and told me to get out as quickly as I could. I stepped out, slipped in the ditch, fell on my back, and rolled over.

Now Captain Libby said, "You better go tell him to take care of those men."

Captain Nash came back to see me and said, "Orderly, those men have gotten liquor someplace and I don't know where. They are so noisy, I wish you would go and take care of them."

Hanning put his rubber blanket over his shoulders, for it was raining very hard, went out and told the men to go into their quarters. The worst one began to put up a fight, but I caught him by the collar and he went headlong. I picked him up and put him in his quarters. When I went back out, two of them were gone. I did not see them anywhere, and I did not look for them. The other two were standing there quietly, and I spoke quite softly to them, "I want you both to get into your quarters now. It is damp out here, and you are going to get sick if you continue to do these crazy things." For once they obeyed.

After this experience, Captain Nash gave an order to some of my men to go and buy a bottle of liquor for themselves. I got hold of this information and went to Nash. I said to him, "Captain, if you give my men any more orders for liquor, I am going to report you if I have to go to General Meade's headquarters."

The next time they wanted whiskey, they went to Sergeant Nickerson to see if he would write them an order. He said, "Go get Hanning to write an order, then I will sign it."

They came to me and wanted me to write an order for two dollars. After they got it and had it signed, they went off to the sutler's shop and presented their order. (A Sutler was a person who followed the Army to sell food, and liquor.)[31]

The sutler wanted to know what the money was for. The men told him they wanted a bottle of whiskey. The salesman said, "I cannot let you have it unless the note is written to show the money is to buy whiskey."

The men came back and asked me to write the note for a bottle of whiskey. I told them, "No Sir, I do not give liquor to a bunch of hoodlums." I guess they decided to give up. They sounded like they had had enough anyway. Before leaving, one of the men stretched out his arms and said, "Sergeant, let me kiss you for I love you."

I told him, "Just you never mind. Get that out of your noggin. You are drunk with liquor and you chew tobacco." I led them all to their quarters and told them to stay there until I called for them. I did not hear anything from them until the next morning.

Sometime after that, during the winter months there was another troublesome man named Abram that got liquor, and his Orderly Sergeant had put him under guard. Abram had not been under guard very long when he walked out past one of the guards and took off. I was eating my supper when two men from his squad came to tell me that he had gotten out and was gone. I said, "Well, go get him. I thought you were a smart lot of fifteen men. How did you let one man get away?"

I thought maybe I better go and see what was going on, and I went to the guard tent to get a guard to go with me. We went up to Abram's Orderly Sergeant's quarters. Abram was there yelling at his Orderly. He said, "Sergeant, Sergeant Hanning is out to get me. I like him, but he doesn't want me."

His Orderly said, "Abram, you had better be careful. You should think about what might happen to you before you go out and get drunk."

Abram said, "I don't care about any other man but him."

Just as he said that, I opened the door and said, "Abram, I want you to come out here." Abram turned and started to run.

I yelled to him, "Abram, halt now!" I told the guard who was with me to fire, but as I said it Abram dropped down on the ground.

Abram said, "Sergeant Hanning, please carry me to the guard tent."

I said to him, "Get up right now. You have two feet, use them. There is nothing wrong with you except you are drunk with liquor." He started moving slowly pretending he needed help. Speaking loudly I said, "Abram, get up now!" He got up and I took hold of his arm. I led him off to the guard tent to put him under guard. He began to act pretty badly. He got his jackknife out and began to tell us what he might do. I said to him, "Give me the knife," but he put it back into his pocket. I walked over to him and sharply said, "You give it to me." He took it right out and gave it to me. I made up a bed and told him to lie down, but he started to climb up the chimney. He fell back into the fire and burned himself and his clothes. Then I took him, put him in the place I fixed for him, laid him down, and he laid there the balance of the night.

The next morning the Lieutenant in his squad reported him, and I reported the Lieutenant because he belonged to my company. He was going to take a month's pay away from Abe because of this escapade. I did not feel this to be an appropriate action, and I felt it best to have the whole thing investigated. The Officials decided to let Abram go.

The fourth day of May 1864 General Grant, the commander of the Army of the Potomac, gave orders to be ready to move at twelve o'clock that night. It was ten o'clock when we got the orders. I had just come in from picket and had turned in for the night. The Captain of my company gave me orders to have the company fall in which I followed. We were to have eight days of rations. We were to put five in the haversack, and three in the knapsack. Each of us was to have forty rounds of cartridges in our cartridge box.

We started at the hour of twelve midnight marching thirty-three miles, with the exception of thirty minutes to get breakfast in the morning. After we crossed the Rappahannock River, we never made another halt until we gained our position at Chancellorsville. Our regiment bivouacked one year to the day after the Second Fredericksburg fight that was on the fourth day of May 1863.

We arrived at Wilderness around two o'clock in the afternoon, and the next day we went searching to find the enemy. We did not hunt long before we found them and we were engaged in battle at three o'clock. We lost heavily. One thing I will say about this engagement, I had the bottom of my haversack shot out losing all the balance of my rations. We lay on our arms all night. The next morning we made a charge taking about one and a half brigade of Rebels as prisoners. While on this charge, just as I was stepping up off the bank of the road I was wounded in the head. That ended my fighting.

This happened on May 6, 1864. The bullet struck me in the forehead and seriously wounded me. I was insensible when my old Brigade Commander H. Hobert Ward came up to see me. He knew who I was and told his Orderly, "Get him on your horse and take him to the hospital at the rear."

I could not recollect anything during the first fourteen days. I could not tell what my name was, what regiment I was in, or what company I belonged to until I was told.

They sent me to Meridian Hill Hospital in Washington where I stayed for only two days, because I was beginning to come to myself. From there I was sent to McClellan Hospital in Philadelphia. Doctor Curtis, a private practice doctor in Philadelphia, was the Head Doctor at the hospital. He came into the hospital to examine the wounded. The ward doctor who had already seen me told him about me, for I was on the danger list. Doctor Curtis examined the wound which had previously healed over, but it was all broken out that morning. He said, "The ball went through your skull well up over the right eye, went on the inside of your skull just over your right ear, and lodged in the thick part of your skull in the back of your head. Sergeant Hanning, this is a very serious condition, plus it has become infected and we must clean out the wound and dress it. I will give you some ether, as it will ease the pain."

I replied, "I do not want any ether."

Doctor Curtis said, "You will be much more comfortable if you let me give you some. Are you sure?"

Hanning said, "I am sure."

The two doctors put me in a barber's chair, tried to make me comfortable, and went to work. They probed and finally trappaned it, dressed it, and made a nice job. They did not think I was going to make it. (I am assuming that trappaned means to sterilize the wound and flesh around it before dressing it. They used silver nitrate which was important back in this era, due to it being a germicide and an astringent.)[32] When the doctors put the silver nitrate over the wound, I fainted away twice from the very reason I would not take the ether. The second time I fainted, I came out to consciousness just as I heard Doctor Curtis say, "If he faints the third time he will go. He will not come out of it."

I told the doctors, "I hain't going to." This all happened twenty-one days after I was wounded.

After the surgery they put me on a stretcher, took me out to the ward, and put me on a cot. The Ward Master told me that I laid there for three days without saying or eating anything. Then they started giving me a stimulant and other liquid foods that I could handle. The fourth day they brought me about one half pint of beef tea that I consumed through a glass straw. I drank it all and asked for more. They gave me all that I asked for until I could take solid food. I began to gain strength and I recovered.

Doctor Curtis that did my surgery told the Ward Doctor, "I want to see Sergeant Hanning before he is discharged from the hospital." An appointment was made and we went down to see Dr. Curtis. The old gentleman had a long talk with me. Doctor Curtis said, "Elisha, you had one chance in a thousand of living."

I told Dr. Curtis, "That is the one I took."

He said, "In all of my professional experiences, I have never seen a man that exhibited self will as you have done. That is what saved you." After he changed the dressing on my wound, I shook hands with the doctor and thanked him for what he had done for me.

The Ward Doctor and I returned to the hospital to prepare for my discharge. This was almost the end of June 1864. My enlistment time, for the three years of service, runs out on the twenty-ninth of July and I wanted to go home.

I thought I was going down to Philadelphia to get transportation home, but they sent me to Washington to the Distribution Camp at Arlington, Virginia. I could not find anyone who could help me. Someone said there was some woman that could arrange transportation for me, and I went to see her. She had an Officer in tow and answered me quite short. She told me, "I have no idea how I can help you." I turned around abruptly and walked off.

Getting back to the main office at the Distribution Camp, one of the Orderlies had detailed me to build a fence. I couldn't believe what I was hearing. I said to him, "Why don't you go where they do not rake up fire over night." I left quickly.

I decided to go over to see General Heintzelman who was in command at the Camp. I asked the guard if I could see the General. He went into the office and came back to tell me, "The General told me to admit you."

I thanked the guard and entered the General's office. "General Heintzelman, I am Sergeant Hanning of the Fourth Maine Regiment and I thank you for seeing me. I was just released from McClellan Hospital, and I am trying to find out how I am going to get home."

He caught hold of my hand and shook hands with me. He said, "I recall an article I just read several days ago that said the Fourth Maine Regiment's time was up, and the troops had left the front lines. Sergeant Hanning, thank you for the service you have given our country, and I wish you a speedy recovery. I will see that you get home."

The General said to his Orderly, "Go bring both horses up. I'm going to have you take Sergeant Hanning to Washington. It's only about seven miles up there so it won't take very long."

The General then looked at me and gave me a note. He said, "This tells you where to go once you get to Washington, and they'll see that you get home. The Orderly arrived with the horses at the headquarters of the Command Center, and the General said to me, "Sergeant Hanning, get on that horse, get going, and good luck to you."

I thanked, General Heintzelman, as he waved us good-bye.

When I got to Washington, I finally got my transportation. While I was waiting, I fell in with one of General Ward's aides. He said to me, "General Ward is in Washington now. Would you like to see him?"

"I would really like to see him before leaving. Where is he?"

The aide said, "It will be on your way to the depot. I will get word to him that you will be stopping by to see him." He gave me directions, and I thanked him. Off I went to General Ward's office.

It did not take me very long to arrive. I opened the door and saw General Ward sitting at his desk working. I said, "Hi, General Ward. Thanks for taking the time to see me."

He came to greet me saying, "Sergeant Hanning, this is one special day for me. Welcome, and it is a pleasure to see you again. The day you were wounded when I told my Orderly to get his horse and take you to the Field Hospital, I never expected to see you again. How are you feeling?"

"General Ward, I am doing very well. Thank you and I appreciate you seeing me today. When I found out you were in Washington, I had to see you to tell you how thankful I am for what you did for me that day. Some of the men told me later, the Rebels held the ground where I laid within one half hour after you got me out of there. I wanted to say a big thank you to you, for you are the one that saved my life."

"This makes me very happy, Sergeant, because there were so many I couldn't help. I appreciate your coming to see me. You are one of the lucky ones to be going home, for so many didn't make it. I just heard the Fourth Maine Regiment was at the depot, and they are leaving tonight," General Ward said.

"I'm on my way to the depot now so I'll probably see them when I get there. I'm sure glad you were in Washington so I could see you. Many thanks again and by the way, congratulations on your promotion to General. You really deserved it." We shook hands and said goodbye. I left for I was going home.

It was another short hop to the depot where I found my buddies, and we all went to Baltimore, Maryland, on the same train. Once we got to Baltimore I told the crew I had to leave them, as my ticket was different. I left the Regiment and went on my own hoof, as my transportation was for New York, but once there and waiting for my train to Boston, I looked up and said, "My gosh! Here come my buddies again. Look guys, I don't have a whole lot of time, but let's go have a quick cup of coffee."

Our tongues were a-wagging for about twenty minutes, as we were all so excited to be this close to getting home. My time was up, and I said, "My friends, I gotta go. You know we'll all be together again in a few weeks, so we can have a good visit then. See you in Rockland, if not before." Waving good-bye, I turned and left to catch my train to Boston.

I made it to Boston early the next morning. I was on my own from here on, so I went to Augusta, Maine, where I could catch a stage coach across the country forty miles to Belfast. I was finally home!

I went to my old boarding house at about two o'clock in the morning and woke the lady up when I rang the doorbell. She came to the door wanting to know who was there. I said, "This is Charles Hanning."

She replied, "It cannot be possible for he was reported dead."

"Well," I told her, "I am the livest dead man you will ever see, for it is me."

She had two daughters, young ladies who got up to see what was going on. As soon as they got downstairs they said, "Mother, it's Uncle Hanning, we know his voice," so she opened the door and found no trouble in recognizing me. There was quite a hustle for a little while.

The girl's mother told them, "You girls are going to smother Uncle Charles to death. He's probably very tired so just sit quietly next to him." They snuggled in beside me, but it was sometime before they would let go of me. I looked natural even though my head was all bandaged. They rushed out to the neighbors to tell them the news. The ones that lived the nearest had woken up and heard what was going on, and they rushed into the boarding house to see me. The house was filled to overflowing with my friends. About daylight I laid down to get a little nap, but I did not lay long for there were still people coming to see me. I had to get up and dress. About eight o'clock I went uptown. Most everyone had found out that I had gotten home, but some of the town folks wanted to know if I was brought home in a box. They had seen in the newspaper that I was dead. They were really surprised to see me resuscitated and looking so good.

The town's people said to me, "You are a pretty live dead man, and we are really glad to have you back home with us."

"I'm feeling very blessed and lucky to be back with everyone too, for the doctors did not hold out much hope for me."

I think this was the third day of July 1864. Everyone in town was expecting the Fourth Maine Regiment home that day. After I had seen the folks in town, I thought I would go and see my fair haired girl, Roxana, who was the one I wanted to see most of all. There was a nice man that took me to his buggy and carried me up to her house, about a mile away very near to where her father lived.

My girl had gone over to see her neighbor, Mrs. Wright, and when she went in the neighbor was crying. Roxana asked, "Why are you crying?"

Her neighbor said, "Have you not heard the news?"

Roxana said, "No, what has happened?"

Mrs. Wright showed her the paper, but before she had time to read about my being dead, her neighbor started screaming. "Roxana, look! There's Charles in the carriage out in front of your house. He has come home."

They both rushed over to the carriage. After Roxana had given me a big smooch and a hug, Mrs. Wright grabbed me, hugged me, and said, "Oh Charles, I am so glad to see you are home with us. What a wonderful day this is."

Roxana asked, "Mrs. Wright, why were you crying when I got to your house?"

Mrs. Wright said, "I had just finished reading the article in the paper about Charles Hanning's death.

Roxana said, "I'm sure glad I did not have a chance to read it."

After my friends had seen me with my head all bandaged up, I tried to settle down before going to see my two children who were living in the country about six miles from town. They had heard I was dead and they had had their cry.

That afternoon the girls saw several of the neighbor boys returning home from the war. The girls asked them about my being dead. The boys answered, "We guess not, because we just saw him about an hour ago before we left town. He is as live a man as we have seen. He was visiting with all of the town folks and you could tell he was happy to be home."

The next day I went out to see my children and be with them for a few days. I could tell they were happy to have me at home with them. On the nineteenth of July 1864 those of us who served and were lucky enough to get home, gathered and went to Rockland, Maine, to be mustered out of the service for the Civil War.

We did offer to form a battery. We telegraphed the Governor in Augusta, Maine to tell him we would continue fighting to protect our country. He immediately got back to us and said, "Yes, we need all the help we can get."

We elected our Officers and among the thirty-four in number, I got thirty-two votes to be Captain. About one hour later we got a dispatch that we could not be accepted as a battery, but they would accept us as Infantry. None of us wanted to serve as Infantry again, so we disbanded. This was finally the end of fighting for us all.

I was three years and three months in the service. The war lasted nine months after that.

(There were a total of 1440 men from Belfast and Knox County companies who served a three-year term in the Fourth Maine Volunteer Infantry Regiment. There were 347 that did not make it home. They were either killed in action, died of disease while in prison, or expired after being seriously wounded. Of the 1093 men returning to Maine, 443 of them had survived wounds.)[33]

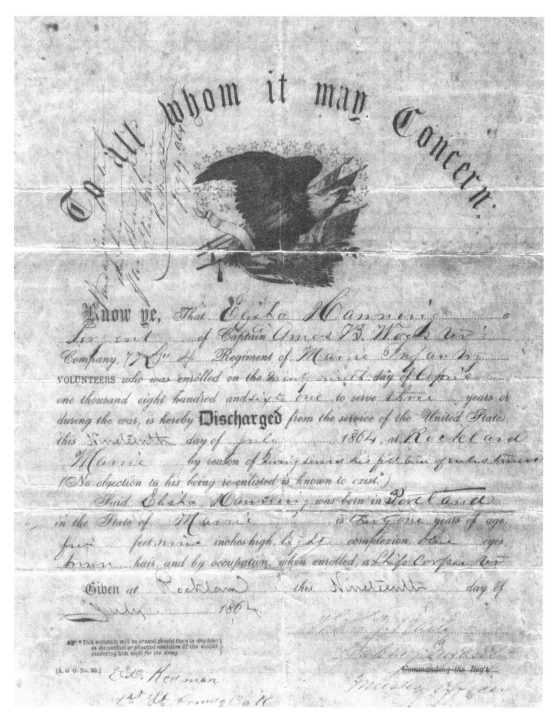

Hanning's Civil War Discharge paper.

AFTER THE WAR 1864-1884

My life started over once again during the rest of 1864. As I have stated in my writings when I had time off from sailing, I often did different kinds of work building new vessels. It was the beginning of September. I was no longer fighting a war, and I needed to find work. I went down to East Boston to the Charlestown Navy Yard to see if I could get any. I was very lucky to get a job immediately that paid four dollars per day. (The Charlestown Navy Yard name was changed to the Boston Navy Yard sometime before 1890. It was later changed to Boston Naval Shipyard and placed on the U.S. National Register of Historic Places, November 15, 1966.)[34]

After a month on the job, I decided to go down to Belfast and get married. (Charles Elisha Hanning and Roxana W. Weymouth were married on November 8, 1864, in Boston, Massachusetts.) We were able to find a room in a nice boarding house in Charleston for the winter months.

During the spring of 1865 we found a nice house to rent. My children could now join us, and we went to keeping house. The girls were now twelve and ten years old. My wife was very fond of them and they thought a great deal of her. She did not have any children of her own, but everybody thought the girls were hers because they looked so much like her.

In the summer my old agent, that I had sailed vessels for, came after me to go to Liverpool, England, to get a ship they had turned the Captain out of. I sailed with her about a year and a half, but she was sailing under an English register and I did not like it. The owners sold her to an English house. When I got home, I got my old position in the Navy Yard back and worked there about three more years.

Then my brother-in-law wanted me to take charge of putting a sugar deck on his barque, the *General W. J. Sherman*, so I left the Navy Yard and went to Philadelphia. We started work as soon as I got settled in, and it was quite an experience. I talked to the boss, where the vessel was moored, about the work and how I wanted it done. He was to get the materials and men together for me. There were five men that came to work the first day, and they started right in tearing the deck all to pieces. I told them, "This is not the way this work is to be done. Did not the boss tell you how I wanted it done?"

"He just told us we had a deck to repair, and we better get started tearing the old one off," one of them said.

Then I explained exactly how I wanted it done.

Another one said, "We do things differently than that."

I said, "If you are going to work here you better listen to how I want it done." Then I asked them, "Where is the lumber and other materials we need? The boss was suppose to have the materials here before you started work."

One of them said, "There was not any lumber ordered."

I said, "What are you going to work with?"

One of them replied, "We came to tear out so we could get it ready."

I said, "I want you to fetch the lumber first. When it gets here, I will tell you again what I want you to do and how it should be done."

They went back and reported to the boss that there was nothing for them to do until the lumber got there. He came aboard in a blustering way.

The boss asked, "What's going on here? The men tell me there is nothing for them to do. Just what do you want done?"

"I want the lumber here before any work is started. Then you can send the men back."

The boss said, "I thought the men had to tear the deck out before you would be ready for the lumber!"

Hanning said, "I told you what I wanted, and I want it if you are going to do the job. Then you can send your men on board to work."

"I sent the men." the boss said.

"Did you send them to sit here and wait on expenses until the lumber came?" I was getting a little hot under the collar.

The boss told me, "There is work enough to do until I can get the lumber here."

"I know exactly what there is to do and how it should be done. I will get someone else if you cannot do it. Do you understand what I am saying or not?," says I.

The boss said, "If I knew what you wanted done I would have done it."

Hanning said, "Look at the statement I made out for you."

"It's in the office," said the boss on the job.

Hanning said, "Is that the way you do business? Take a statement, lay it away in a drawer, and then do as you have a mind to? You have got to do just as I want you to do, or I will take the vessel and go to Boston."

The boss on the job finally told me he would order the lumber, and the men will come back on the job when it arrives. The lumber was finally delivered. Two of the men came and said they were ready to go to work. I showed them exactly what I wanted done and they got started, but one worked about a half hour and went away. Then in about a half hour the other one left. They were both gone about an hour and a half to two hours. Then they came back.

I asked them, "What have you been doing?"

The men said, "That's none of your business."

I said, "Well it is, and you get ashore just as quickly as you can. I don't put up with slothful workers."

They quickly went ashore, but just as fast as they went the boss arrived and wanted to know what the trouble was all about now. I told the boss exactly what went on. Then I said, "I have recorded the time they were here, and that is all they will be paid for. You need not send those two back here.

I will give you one more chance to get started on this work. If it does not work out I will clear for Boston. I want some good men here by one o'clock to work."

The men did not arrive until a quarter to two. I sent them back, went up to the agent and cleared for Boston. When I got back on board the vessel the boss was there, and I told him I had had enough.

There was one very large fellow that came back with him, and when I was telling the boss the reason I was leaving, the big man said, "You are a d--- liar. We were here at one o'clock." Immediately he felt the end of my arm and went heels over head. When he got up, he had his hand on his face and was making for the wharf.

Having cleared the vessel for Boston, I said to the boss, "You can take your lumber away and make out your bill for one and a half hours work."

He replied, "I will attach the vessel for full pay."

I told him, "Go ahead. I have engaged the tug to tow me out tomorrow morning to Fort Richmond to load with coal for Boston."

The boss said, "I will do the work and do as you want it done. I will come here myself and see that the men are here on time." Hoping I could take his word seriously, I cancelled the tug and clearance of the vessel for the next day.

He followed through on his promise. Early the next morning six men and the boss were there starting on the work. They did as I asked, did a nice job, and finished it in short order. The carpenter's work on the deck was finished except for the caulkers. I went through the same thing with them when they came, for they were going to do it their way. I discharged them and went to the boss. He said he would be down with some good men at 10 o'clock to work and finish things up. They all came on time, worked all day, and by six o'clock that night the job was finished. They had done a very good job. I told the boss to make out his bill, and we would take care of it at nine o'clock in the morning.

He presented his bill to me when he arrived on time. He had full time for all hands, and I gave him a copy of my records which showed him the men who had been on board working with their arrival and departure times. Comparing them, we found there were five days difference.

I told him, "I will not pay this. I do not owe you this much."

The boss said, "I will put a lien on the vessel."

"Go ahead, but if you do that I'll get bonds," I said.

The boss quickly changed his tune. He said, "I will split the difference with you. We'll call it two and a half days difference."

"Nothing doing, you settle with my bill. I've had to put up with too many problems while I have been here," says I.

He said he would settle using the bill l presented, and I paid him for his services. He told me to be careful about being around town, because the men were not happy with me.

I told the boss, "Tell them they better bring an undertaker with them if any of them are thinking of doing harm." I did not meet with any trouble.

I loaded the vessel with coal, got hold of the Captain, and told him his vessel was all ready to sail to Pensacola, Florida.

Then I had another brother-in-law who got into Baltimore, send for me to come and take his vessel to Portland, Maine, with a load of coal. I accepted this voyage because it was a short one. When I got to Portland, the Captain of the ship was there to sail her back home. I took the coach back. I'm beginning to realize just how nice it is to have a home to go home to.

It is now 1869 and we are living in Charlestown, but shortly we moved to East Boston and went to keeping boarders on Meridian Street. This location was between Central Square and London Street. The girls were much older now, but they wanted to come with us to know where we were going to be. They stayed about two weeks and helped us get settled. They both loved the quaintness of the New England states of Maine, Vermont, and Massachusetts, and returned to the state of their choice. Emma and Ellen were both married within a few years.

After I got the house running, I went and laid the launching ways for an iron brig that was launched sideways. After I got the ways finished, I started work on the deck and met with an accident. I fell twenty-three feet into a hole and it laid me up for quite a while. When I got to feeling better, I went back and helped finish the brig. She was built to carry molasses in bulk. Captain Grusting Havener commanded her. After she sailed, I continued my work as a carpenter building vessels.

Mr. Snow and Sons of Boston wanted me to take a schooner to Rio de Janeiro. I refused and they told me if I would take her they would build me any kind of a vessel that I wanted when I returned. I wanted to dreadfully, but my wife would not let me go and I gave in to her.

We had the boarding house for about one and a half years, but got burned out in the big fire of East Boston in 1870. We lost everything in the fire. Fortunately I was insured. We went over to Boston proper and opened another boarding house on Essex Street where we stayed a year and a half until 1872. I was very fortunate to sell this boarding home to a good fireman.

I thought maybe I would try working at various businesses other than building vessels. I first went into the grocery business in Malden, a suburb of Boston. My business was not so fortunate and I lost heavily. My next adventure was in Real Estate, and I was quite successful the first year, but the panic times started to come on, and I lost about eighteen hundred dollars carrying second mortgages. I quickly decided to give up that business. Then I went back in the grocery business again for a short time and did quite well. I began to feel these businesses were a little risky, for I was losing money as quickly as I made it. I started looking for something better to do.

I found a rather interesting job in the firm Fonfield and Foerstall and Co. on Devonshire Street. They employed me for about a year and then they failed, but while I was with them there was a deal made with a firm in Philadelphia. This company owed them about fifteen thousand dollars, and they wanted me to go to Philly to see if I could collect it. When I went into their office and showed them my credentials, their comment was, "We cannot possibly do anything for you."

I asked them, "When will you be able to help me?"

They replied, "We just don't know when that will be."

"I have some ways to discuss this situation with you and I want some satisfaction," says I.

They said, "We have given you all the satisfaction you will get from us." Then they asked me to leave.

I said to them, "If you are thinking of putting me out, you have a real problem on your hands. It will be a big job." Finally I went out, but I told them, "You'll hear from me very soon."

I went out on the street and walked around several blocks to see if I could find what I was looking for. On the third big building across the street, I looked up and saw a sign that said, Attorney at Law. This is it! I went into the attorney's office and had a consultation with him, telling him what I wanted. After he got all of the information out of me that he felt he needed, he said, "I am very sorry, but I am retained as council for those parties, so I will not be able to help you."

I flew into the air and asked, "Why didn't you tell me this before?"

He said, "My friend, don't get too excited here. Just maybe you came to the right place." He gave me a sealed note to give to another law firm where there were two young men that were lawyers. I left not knowing what to do. I almost thought of committing suicide. Finally I found their office, and I handed the note to the one that greeted me. He read the note and made a remark to his partner. I didn't know what to think, and I was getting a little nervous. He finally asked me, "What are you thinking of doing?"

I told them, "I have come to you to consult about where I should go with this situation."

"Well," says one of the Lawyers, "We should put a keeper right in the store." (Keeper: a person who is legally responsible to guard or watch another person's property.)[35]

We talked the matter over and one of them said to the other, "You make out the attachment papers for Captain Hanning and I will go over and see the Sheriff."

All arrangements were made around half past eleven in the morning, and the lawyer and I went into the store with two keepers. In a few minutes the Sheriff came in, inquired about several items he could use, looked them over carefully, and asked about the price of the items he was pretending he needed. When we saw the Sheriff was there, the Lawyer and I went into their office. I told them, "I have returned again."

The owners groaned, "It is no use. We told you, you are barking up the wrong tree when you were here before."

Feeling a bit more secure with the help of my Lawyer, I replied, "I think it is of some importance to me even if it is not to you. I have an attachment here, and the Sheriff is in the store right now to close it up." Then they got up on their feet, went into their back office, and deliberated this situation. This was a dilemma for them for I think we had them between a rock and a hard place.

They came out of the back office and asked, "How about splitting the agreement with us?"

"I will have the whole or none," I said in a strong manner.

Then the store owners wanted to know, "Will you take a cheque on a Wall Street Bank in New York?"

I said, "Yes, if there is enough to cover it. What's the name of the bank?"

The store owners wrote out the cheque and handed it to me. The cheque had the name of the bank on it so my question was answered. I said, "Thank you," and all five of us walked out of the store. My lawyer and I immediately went and telegraphed the bank to find out if there was money to cover the cheque of this company. I asked the banker, "Would you hold it subject to a cheque until eleven o'clock tomorrow morning?"

"Yes," was his answer and he told me there are sufficient funds to cash it.

The lawyer and I went back to his office and I told the both of them, "I sure am glad I was sent to you men. You have been a big help to me and I appreciate it." We settled up and off I went to New York.

The next day I was in the New York Bank with my cheque and there were several parties that recognized me. The Banker wondered if I wanted cash or a cheque. I told him, "I would rather have a Cashier's cheque made out to our Boston Bank, and they wrote out the cheque on the Franklin Bank we used for business. Before returning to Boston, I went to Providence, Rhode Island, to take care of some business for the firm. Our store was closed when I arrived, and I went to my home in East Boston.

The first thing the next morning I went over to Devonshire Street to the store. Mr. Fonfield was there reading the morning paper. He looked up and said, "Good morning, Mr. Hanning." He cast his eyes downward saying, "You didn't have any luck, did you?"

I said, "How do you know?"

"Well," says he, "They have failed."

With a big smile on my face, I said, "I don't care if they have," and I handed him the cheque.

He read it and screamed as loud as he could holler. He held the cheque up and shook it. Then all the men in the store came running to the office to see what had happened. I had to get hold of Mr. Fonfield to help him stand up, and several of the men took my place. Says I, "I think he's gone mad (into shock) and I don't want him to faint."

In a short time we were able to get him cooled down. Then I told the men that I had gotten the cheque and they started yelling. Mr. Fonfield said to me, "You are the only man in the whole world that could have pulled this off."

I told Mr. Fonfield, "You might not be satisfied yet, for I had to pay sixty dollars to the Lawyers I went to see. I gave them each twenty dollars for their help. I gave just as much money to the first one I saw as I did to the ones that did all the work for me. If it hadn't been for him, I would not have known where to go."

Mr. Fonfield remarked, "I really don't care, Mr. Hanning, you could have given them five hundred a piece, and it would have been all right with me. Gosh, I still don't know how you pulled this one off. Good for you!"

Mr. Fonfield and I walked over to the bank and deposited the money. To my surprise, he gave me a very nice bonus. I continued trying to collect outstanding debts with those people we had done business with, but I had very poor luck.

The time had come for me to return to my old business of repairing vessels in East Boston. I owned somewhat in navigation. I had an interest in four, three masted schooners, and there was a Captain Nickerson that wanted me to take an interest in another one called the *Belle Holliday*. I took a thirty-second interest in her. She was a very fine sailing vessel, but she was quite old. Captain Nickerson had been sailing in her for about a year and got into a wreck. Someone ran into the vessel, and we had to repair her. I was asked to take charge of the work, and we had her repaired in first class shape. She was then rated A1, and she could sail for five more years.

Throughout the time spent repairing the vessel, the Captain got very important and began to put on quite an air. I told him, "You had better come down off your high horse, as I'm not going to put up with any of your arrogance." That seemed to only make him worse. He had hired me to take charge of the work, but all of a sudden he decided he was going to take charge. He went to ordering the men around and telling them what to do. I said to the men, "Do not take any notice of him. I will tell you what needs to be done." This happened early in the forenoon.

The Captain overheard what I said and he replied, "Hanning, I am giving you an order to get off the vessel and if you don't I'll see that you are put off."

I told him, "If you are thinking of doing it you had better commence, for it will take you the balance of the day to do it." He came up to me and caught hold of me. I walloped him on his noggin and thumped his head against the casing. I don't know what I would have done to him if the carpenters had not interfered by getting me off of him. I was mad, but usually I don't get quite so fierce. This time he really struck a chord in me. He got up and went ashore himself, and I finished up the vessel.

Once finished, I went to Captain Nickerson's vessel to get the bills we accumulated during the restoration. I asked him for copies of all the bills, and he told me, "When I get them all, I will give them to you." I waited two days before going back to him. The vessel was gone when I got over to where it had been moored. I found out he was sailing to Chester, Pennsylvania. While he was gone, he got in another wreck and there were bills for those repairs. It was very late in the fall and the Captain evidently decided to winter the vessel in Bristol, Rhode Island, as he did not return to Boston until the next spring.

It was time to confront Captain Nickerson about the bills again, but being so evasive about giving them to me, I decided to talk to Mr. Smith, my attorney first. After explaining my situation to Mr. Smith, he voiced his opinion saying, "I think we should go and talk this over with Captain Nickerson."

The two of us walked over to where the vessel was moored for the summer, hopped on the gang plank, got on board, went to the Captain's quarters and knocked on his door.

The Captain opened the door, looked at us and said, "What are you two doing on my vessel? Get out of here right now!"

Shaking his head Mr. Smith said, "You don't have any idea why we are here. Won't you at least let us tell you?"

"I really don't care why you are here, but I do know I want you off my vessel right now." The slippery Captain said.

My attorney answered with, "Captain, I would suggest you listen to what I have to say or I might have to get hold of the Sheriff."

A nasty answer came from the Captain, "Are you deaf? Leave this vessel immediately!"

I spoke up and told my attorney, "It is all right. Come and we'll get a warrant for his arrest." We left the vessel peacefully without further ado.

This was the only thing left to do. We hoofed it down to the Sheriff's department, summoned an officer, and got a warrant for the Captain's arrest. Officer Joe and I went looking for the Captain, but we couldn't find him anywhere. Evidently he was sulking around town all afternoon, because we had met several people who had seen him. They told us he didn't look very happy. Just at nightfall we got on his track and found him on Commercial Street in Mr. Burse's store. The Officer presented the warrant to him and he said, "What are you going to do to me?"

The Officer replied, "It is entirely up to you. I won't do anything to you, and I'm quite sure you know what this is all about."

Captain Nickerson in his hefty voice said, "I won't do anything or give anything to Hanning."

The Officer said, "Then you will go to the Charles Street jail with me." The Officer pulled out handcuff's to contain Nickerson, tried to put them on him, but Nickerson began to put up a fight.

Suddenly Nickerson stopped being so wild. When the handcuffs came out, he looked like there was a pack of wolves after him. He looked sacred to death, and I noticed his knees were beginning to buckle from under him. He was no longer trying to fight Officer Joe and said, "I want to know what I can do to get this beast off my back."

Officer Joe said to him, "Well, it really isn't my job to advise you, but you can get yourself a lawyer if you want to."

Nickerson replied, "I'll go get one right now."

The Officer told him, "I cannot allow you to do that, but you can send for one."

Nickerson spotted a friend in the store, "Sammy, I need a lawyer. Please go and engage one for me and bring him back here."

Sammy and an attorney came back in about an hour. While we were waiting, there were three Captains with whom I was acquainted in the store having coffee. We had a general shaking of hands and talked the matter over. I told them what the trouble was, and they all felt Nickerson was a fool. Two of them told him so right to his face.

When the attorney arrived, he told the Captain he would have to give bonds or go to jail. The

Sheriff fixed his bonds to appear in court the next day. Scheduling for the case was about four weeks out before he was to appear in court. He finally produced the bills, and I found he had used almost five hundred dollars of the vessel's money. As he was captain of the vessel and part owner, and I was a partner, I could not sue him for my part of the money. I had to carry this in a court of equity, and that would eat my part of the vessel up. I had to give that up.

Captain Nickerson went on another trip and thought he had the best of me, but I decided to go and see a friend of mine, Mr. D. C. Mayo. He advised me to go and see John C. Dodge, a commercial lawyer. I laid my case before him and he advised me not to go in a court of equity. John told me, "There is a new law that was enacted about nine years ago that very few commercial men know about. You can liable the vessel for one, three, or five years, and if she is lost during that time or damaged in any way, the rest of the owners will be responsible for it. You will have to get three carpenters to appraise her to see what she is worth, and the rest of the owners will have to pay you what she was appraised at."

I told one of the owners what I was going to do, and he asked me to wait a couple of hours. He said, "I want to go and see James Menrow, one of our other part owners before you do that."

I told him, "I really don't want to wait, but if you will go right now, I'll give you some time to go and see him. Please hurry." He got back in about an hour and wanted to know what I would take for my part of ownership in the vessel. I figured up what I had paid out on her, charged six percent for the money Nickerson had spent, and told him what he could pay for my part of the ownership. He told me to make out a bill of sale and he would pay me for my interest in the vessel. I went to my lawyer's office, got the necessary legal papers to sell my share, and went to my partner. He wrote out a cheque for the asking price, gave it to me, and that ended my investment very favorably.

I owned in another three masted vessel called *William H. White* that my brother-in-law, Captain George B. Ames sailed in. Word was sent to me that when he got into New York from his last trip, he was very sick and had to go the hospital. He wanted me to come and take care of the ship. I discharged her and stayed with him until he got well. While I was there, I sold my part of her which was thirty two shares. For that transaction, I collected all of the cost I had spent on her plus the interest I had paid. That was a pretty good deal too. I also sold my sixteenth interest in another three masted schooner that I owned in and got my money for her.

When I got home, I had some money on hand, but I did not want to invest any more in navigation. I talked with my wife and she suggested I get rid of the rest of my investments in navigation and go into real estate business.

I told her, "Roxana, I sold everything out when I was in New York." She owned a sixteenth interest in a vessel and wanted me to sell that for her. I told her, "This is not a good time to sell any interest you might have in that vessel, because you cannot get anything near what she is worth. You had better keep her for awhile."

"Well all right, but you know Charles, I have been thinking while you were gone that maybe we should go down on the Cape and build a house for our retirement. If you want to, we can buy up some extra land and maybe make some money on it." Then she suggested, "Onset would be a nice place to go. It is the gateway to Cape Cod and has been the Spiritual Camp Meeting grounds for a number of years."

That sounded like a good idea to me. December 1883 we started building our little cottage in Onset, and on the first day of June 1884 we moved to Onset.

(Wareham, Plymouth County, Massachusetts, is in the southeastern section of the state. This area was formally known as the "Agawam Plantation" and included many small villages. The land was purchased from the Native owners in 1665. Onset was one of those villages. It was purchased through a "…Special charter…applied for to the Massachusetts Legislature," and granted March 31, 1877. It is located on a tranquil bay with sandy white beaches, and is a favorite vacation spot for many families.)[36]

LIFE IN ONSET 1884-1907

Arriving in Onset Bay to our home on Colony Road, I spent a little time fixing up the landscaping outside while Roxana worked inside. Her health had been declining while living in Boston, and I knew she felt better down here. It was probably the good fresh air.

The first thing I did living there, once the house was all finished, was to go into the teaming and livery business. I heard they were going to build a horse railroad between Onset Junction, in East Wareham, and Onset. The horsecar railroad was a southerly extension connecting to the Old Colony Railroad that stopped in Wareham before going on to Cape Cod. Several men came and asked me to take stock in the road and wondered if I would be on the Board of Directors. I told them, "I would very much like to be a member." One of the men, who was a carpenter, and I took one-half share each with the understanding that we would take three or four more if everything was satisfactory. They had a meeting to elect officers and they ignored letting us know. I found out what had gone on at the meeting, and I was upset they had not included us, for we each paid fifty dollars for our half share.

While getting everything ready to start the road, the president Thomas B. Griffice, came to me and asked, "Will you help us figure out how much lumber it is going to take and how many sleepers we will need for this project?"

My reply was quite sharp telling him, "I will not do anything more to help when you cannot even notify your Board Members of meetings. Also, in the few conversations you and I have had, I find out you have lied to me. I'm done with you."

Griffice said, "This was a bad mistake that we made."

I told him, "There was no mistake made. There was a lie made."

He said, "You know, I took you to be a different kind of man."

I told him, "I suppose you took me for a fool, but I took you to be a truthful man. I am not a fool and I have found out you are a notorious liar."

Griffice started across the street but came back and said, "This was all a mistake. I do not want to break up our friendship, and I am going to call another meeting and have the former meeting annulled." This was Saturday and he told me, "I will call the meeting for next Monday night."

We decided that we would get together and go over all the affairs concerning the road. Monday he wanted to consult again and I cooperated. Monday night came and went and there was never any notice given to me to attend the meeting. I saw the President on Tuesday, and he did not say one word about what went on at the Monday night meeting.

The next day I got a letter from East Boston. They wanted me to come up to take charge of some ship work, so on Thursday Roxana and I packed up our things and went to Boston. We were on the coach and guess who we saw sitting in the back! None other than Thomas B. Griffice and another board member. He wanted to make talk with me about some work he needed done on his house.

I told him, "There are men out there that will do that for you. I do not want any of your work. I think you should go to where they do not rake up any fire over night."

My wife asked me, "Who is that man you were talking to that way?"

I said, "That is old Thomas Griffice." She did not know him by sight, and they did not have anything more to say to me.

When we arrived at one of the depots on the stops, Griffice sent the Chairman of the Selectmen to inquire where I was going. I told him, "I'm going crazy. Want to come along?" We got aboard for the next stop in Tremont, about seven miles farther, and no more questions were asked. They didn't even want to meet my wife who was with me. This made me wonder just what kind of people were going to run the horsecar railroad. Would they succeed or fail? They were only interested in themselves and what they could get out of others.

We got into Boston on April seventeenth and stayed until the end of June. We wanted to return to Onset in time for the Fourth of July Celebrations. While I was there, I got a pretty good handle on the work they wanted done, and I really got kind of excited about being able to do carpentry work again. I guess it's in my blood. We were able to locate some very good men to help, and I got most of the materials and supplies lined up, so we could get to work immediately when I returned. I also was able to visit with and get to know the men that would be working with me. I liked them all. This was a pleasure after some of my experiences during the years.

After our Fourth celebrations were over, I got ready and returned to Boston. Before leaving Onset, I was lucky to sell the half share of railroad stock that I paid fifty dollars for, to a man that paid me ten dollars. He paid the balance and got his share for sixty dollars. I jokingly told him, "Now I have ten dollars for my half-share, but you will never receive a quarter of the ten dollars you gave me, nor the other fifty dollars you spent."

The men were all waiting for me when I got to Boston. They couldn't wait to get to work. I barely had time to find a room and get myself organized. With everyone's help we started working the day after I got back. What a group of men I had! Each man knew what his job was, got to work, and did a great job the entire year we were together. There was absolutely not one harsh word spoken during this time. If anyone on the team needed help with something, someone was right there to help. I was almost sorry to see the end in site. This was a great way to end my carpentry work on vessels.

During the year Roxana came up several times to spend a few weeks with me. With the long hours we spent working, it was wonderful going home to a good home cooked meal and be with my gal. I went back to Onset with six hundred dollars clear of all expenses.

While I was gone, the horsecar railroad had started running between Onset and Onset Junction. A friend of mine put one coach with two horses on the railroad. He was having good success getting passengers away from the horsecars, but he didn't like the way he was being treated by the men who ran the cars or the owners of the horse railroad. He was continuously harassed by these folks and he gave up after forty days.

It was early June when I got back to Onset, and l told my friend who had been run off by the owners, "I will advance you seven hundred dollars to buy a span of horses and several coaches. Run them in opposition to the horsecars and I will help you." He did not want to. I went and bought my own horses and a large coach. I started running them myself. The first time I went up to the depot in Onset Junction, I carried nine passengers. The horsecars did not get any. On the way back I brought fourteen passengers home. That was a Saturday and that night I got three dollars to carry a party home from a dance. The next morning I went to the Onset Junction Depot with my team and took a full load of passengers down to Onset. There were so many people, they hung on wherever they could. We had no room to carry their trunks, and I had to go back up and get them later. The horsecars had only four people.

When we arrived in Onset, President Griffice greeted us and was raging mad. He told me, "We drove the other fellow off in forty days. We will drive you off in twenty."

My friend that was run off by Griffice and his men was on my coach and said, "Mr. Griffice, you are badly mistaken. Do you know anything about Hanning?"

Griffice said, "Nothing more than I am acquainted with him."

My friend said, "Well, I have been talking with a man who has known him all of his life, and he told me you can depend on the fact that Hanning has come to stay."

After this confrontation ended, I turned around and went back up to Onset Junction to get the trunks. I found that several officials of the railroad had gone over to the Depot Master and bought him off. He would not deliver the trunks to me. I took my baggage checks and went into the baggage room.

The Depot Master came right over and said, "I forbid you from taking these trunks. I will report you to the Road Officials for making trouble."

I told him, "You had better go pack up your things, for I don't think your service will be needed any longer."

He replied, "I guess you will find out you cannot come here any longer."

I started after him, but he ran into his office and locked himself in. I got my trunks, gave my checks to the freight agent, and took off for Onset. By the way, the freight agent was a very nice man.

While I was getting the trunks, evidently President Griffice had gone to the Old Colony Official and asked, "Can't you drive this Hanning creature away from the depot?"

The Official replied, "The depot is a public place for everybody."

Griffice asked, "Can't you stop him from collecting baggage?"

"We can stop him from soliciting, but if anyone wants him to carry their baggage he cannot be stopped."

Another friend over-heard this conversation and told me what had been said. I decided I was not going to put up with any deceitfulness. I wrote a letter to the Superintendent of the Onset Junction Depot stating what the Depot Master had done and immediately mailed it. The next morning when I arrived at the depot, Mr. Griffice, the Superintendent, the Depot Master, and the freight agent were all there. My letter was on the desk.

The Superintendent asked me, "What is going on here to create such a problem?"

I quickly answered, "Will you please read the letter."

He opened the letter and read it out loud. The Depot Master and a lot of passengers were standing on the platform. Everyone heard the letter.

The Superintendent asked the Depot Master, "What do you have to say about this?"

The Depot Master started giving him a very evasive answer, but finally admitted, "It happened just as he has stated it."

"What authority have you to refuse delivering those trunks when the checks were presented?" asked the Superintendent.

The Depot Master told him, "Mr. Griffice told me not to give the trunks to him."

"Do you want this company sued for damages?" replied the Superintendent. "I want you to give me the keys to the baggage room."

"Does this mean you are discharging me?" the Master Depot asked.

"Yes," was the reply. "It does immediately, for you have nothing more to say here."

The Superintendent told the freight agent, "Take the keys and engage a man for your position. I want you to fill the job of Depot Master."

The President of the horse railroad, Mr. Griffice, wanted to make some talk with the Superintendent, but was told, "I have no more time to discuss this petty situation," and off he went.

Griffice was left standing there with his heart broken. The passengers waiting for my coach to take them to Onset started cheering.

My friend, the freight agent, told me, "President Griffice's men are going to do everything they can think of to bother you."

"You can say that again. Perhaps we won't have any more problems. Let's hope not." I said.

When someone started picking on me I would tell them, "Why don't you stop your crazy music right away. I am going to continue with my horse coach, because we are all having a good time and I am not giving it up."

Then the men running the railroad cars got a worthless creature who started meddling with my passengers. They set him up in the shoe shining business at the Onset Depot. When he got on his high-horse and told the passengers they were at the wrong stand, I would go over and tell him, "Go on back to your business, keep your mouth shut, or some day you'll wish you had."

That day was not far off. I made up my mind that I was not going to tolerate him any longer. I picked him up by the seat of his pants and booted him back over to his spot.

He prosecuted me for assault, and I was fined ten dollars. I foolishly appealed the case and paid eighty-five dollars more, but I got rid of him.

My horse coach trolley kept on running until I was ready to give it up.

Another situation I had with the railroad was when the Division Agent, Mr. Taylor, bought a piece of land alongside the railroad for forty-five dollars. Mr. Martin that deeded the property to him did not own the land. Several months before this sale occurred, he had sold it to a widow lady, Mrs. Hammond and deeded it to her. She had recorded the deed. Mr. Martin left the state and went to Connecticut. Fortunately, instead of paying cash for the property, Mrs. Hammond had given Martin a mortgage for one hundred fifty dollars payable in one year.

Before the payment was due, Mrs. Hammond came to me and told me she could not get the money anywhere without paying twenty-five percent interest. I told her she should not pay it. I had heard something about Martin and how crooked he was, and I started doing a little investigating. I started by going to Plymouth to look the title up. I found that Martin had indeed sold this piece of land to the railroad, but he had given Taylor a copy of the deed.

I got hold of Mrs. Hammond and told her the things I had found out and said, "You will not have to pay that kind of interest on any money, and you will not have to pay the mortgage in full. I will settle this for you. Do you know when Martin is coming to collect the payment?"

Mrs. Hammond said, "He told me he would be here between eight and eight thirty Saturday night." Thanks, Mr. Hanning, for helping me."

"When he arrives, tell him that you are meeting at the Notary Public's office and be ready to walk over there. We have to make sure we have a witness and the discharge papers are correct and properly signed. I have all of the preparations done and ready for Saturday night. I will meet you there."

The Officer and I were there when they arrived. When Mr. Martin saw me, he seemed agitated. I asked him, "Do you have the mortgage with you?"

Martin replied, "Yes, I have it with me."

I asked the Notary Public, "Do you have the discharge papers made out for the mortgage?"

He said, "I have it all done."

I took out my pocketbook and asked Martin to sign the discharge papers. Then I began to read the riot act to him. "I am sure you know what you have done. We won't waste time going over it, but I want you to know I have an Officer with a warrant all ready to have you arrested. I have just fifty dollars to give you."

He said, "What have I done?"

I told him, "You have sold property that did not belong to you, and that is a state prison offense."

"Well, I paid Mrs. Hammond for the land," Mr. Martin said.

Says I, "How did you pay her?"

"I got twenty dollars for the land and I gave her fifteen," Martin said.

I said, "Did not the railroad pay you thirty-five dollars for that land? You just told me you only got twenty dollars for it. What do you say about that?"

"I guess I forgot," Mr. Martin said.

My reply was, "Don't you lie to me. I have no more time to fool with you. Either come to my terms or go to the lock-up." Martin began to cry.

Mrs. Hammond called me into another room and said, "We better give him one hundred dollars."

I told her, "No, I won't."

Finally we settled on seventy-five dollars. "You are liable to be arrested by the Old Colony Road for fraud." I told him, "Get out of here as quickly as you can. If it was not for your wife and children, I would have you arrested right now." He left and has never been seen again.

Now that Mrs. Hammond has clear title to the land, and the discharge papers are legal and properly signed, there is no question about who owns the land. She can do anything she wants to do with it, but I did ask her, "Would you like to give the land to the railroad?" She thought it would be a good idea. She really had no use for it after losing her husband.

I went to see Mr. Taylor, the Division Agent, who bought the land for the railroad from Mr. Martin. I told him, "Mr. Taylor, I want you to know there is a big problem concerning the small strip of land you bought from Mr. Martin. The deed you were given is not valid, and the land is not yours."

Mr. Taylor said, "I am not understanding why this was not a legal deal."

I told him, "The answer is simple. Martin sold the land to Mrs. Hammond shortly before he sold it to you."

He asked me, "Are you sure?"

"Yes, I helped her with paying off the mortgage he was carrying. I looked the records over before I paid it, and I found that her deed had been recorded before Martin gave you a deed."

"Well," said Mr. Taylor, "What can I do?"

"There are three things I think you could do. First, you could tear down the fence you put up and give the property back to Mrs. Hammond. You can also get extradition papers, fetch Martin back to Massachusetts and put him in prison, or you can give Mrs. Hammond a small fee for the land. I'm quite sure she will give you a legal deed."

Taylor said, "I think we probably should do the latter. How much do you feel we should pay her?"

"That's totally up to you. It sounds like Martin gave her fifteen dollars after he sold you the land," I said.

"You know Hanning, Martin was very hesitant to give me a deed to the land when I bought it." said Mr. Taylor. "I guess I should have smelled a rat then."

I told him, "I will get the deed fixed for you, if you would like me to."

Taylor said, "If you will do it, I will make it right with you."

I went to Mrs. Hammond and asked her, "Would you like to sell this piece of land to the railroad for a small fee? They would like to have it for safety reasons. It is very close to the tracks."

Mrs. Hammond said, "That's a good suggestion. Let's get this done."

We went to the attorney's office to have him take care of the paperwork for the sale, so that this time it would be legal. After this was finished, I went to Mr. Taylor to give him the legal deed to the property.

The Old Colony Railroad sent Mrs. Hammond a small fee for helping to clear the title of land and to thank her.

Taylor wanted to know, "Where is your bill?"

I told him, "It will be one dollar and seventy-five cents for making out the deed and seventy-five cents for recording it.

Taylor replied, "We certainly owe you something."

I said, "Make things right here at the depot."

Taylor said, "I'll give you two stands just like everyone else has." He gave the Depot Master orders to keep two stands for Hanning. Taylor took a piece of red chalk and marked out where I could have my stands. When other teams would get in my place, I was told to order them out. However, the men running the horse cars were still determined to make things difficult for me and always encroached on my property at the depot.

The Depot Master and I had become good friends, and he went to bat for me. He told these men, "The time has come when Mr. Hanning's spot here at the depot is his. You all have your own area. Get out of his spot and stay out or you will be asked to leave." After this I had no more trouble, and everything went smoothly the rest of the time I was running. This agreement shattered President Griffice's dream.

During the rest of the time that I ran the horse coach, I sold out twice. Both parties failed and I had to put teams on again for the public demanded it. The first time I sold to a man by the name of Medchif. He proved to be a notorious villain, and the public would not patronize him. I was able to set up a good business again, and I stayed with it for two more years. The second sale was to a man whose name was Crowell. He paid only part of the cost and gave me a mortgage on the teams for the balance. He had a partner by the name of Frank Harrison. They ran for one summer and called it quits. Frank was not a trustworthy character. He took the horses, coach, bills, and mortgage papers, and put my property in a building, locked it up, and refused to give it to me. There was nothing else I could do other than to have him arrested and locked up. I got my teams back and I ran the business until I ran all of the horsecars off. Then the Horsecar Railroad sold out to a Trolley Company. I decided not to continue running with them due to old age setting in.

Every year the stockholders wanted to know what they were getting for a dividend, and every year Griffice told them the same thing. "Go to Hanning. Let him tell you. The travelers are patronizing him instead of the railroad." The first year owners of the stock got a two percent dividend, and there was not a stockholder after that first year that ever got a dollar. The railroad ran for fourteen years and it cost twenty-two thousand dollars. They sold it for fourteen hundred with two lots of land.

Previous to my retirement, I dabbled somewhat in Onset real estate. I bought a twenty-acre piece of land between Onset and Wareham. I worked clearing the property and when the work was done, I sold it for thirteen hundred and fifty dollars. The man that bought it paid me four hundred and fifty dollars down, and I took a mortgage for the balance due in two years. Unfortunately he got drunk one night, laid down out in the cold and froze his feet. They had to be amputated and he passed away shortly after that. His name was Edwin Gulliver, and I had to foreclose on the deal. I sold it to his brother who bid on the property, and he paid me two hundred dollars with a mortgage of eleven hundred and fifty dollars. He failed to meet the payments when they came due. I had to foreclose again. The third time it was sold to Mr. Ferinell who bid it in for two hundred dollars, but this time I gave the mortgage to my partner Mr. Porter to hold. I managed these sales so I would get enough back to cover the payment of the principle, interest, taxes, and all the labor I had done on it. That piece of land paid me about nine hundred and forty dollars, and I only paid out two dollars. The new owners have a mortgage for eleven hundred dollars. I really came out smelling like a rose on that deal. I also owned five houses and several lots in Onset.

Now I'll tell you a few things that have been going on in our village of Onset. Many of our residents attend a weekly meeting to discuss any problems that are upsetting them. As a group we discuss the problems as they arise, have input from those attending, and try to solve the problem together that evening. Sometimes it takes longer. At one of the meetings I brought up the fact that our town of Wareham was twenty-seven thousand dollars in debt. You should have heard the moans and groans with that statement. We decided that something must be done about this, but this problem could not be solved in one evening. One of the members spoke up and asked, "Will you be our village representative and attend their meetings?"

I responded by saying, "I will be very happy to represent Onset, but I feel that the people who are not here tonight should be able to voice their opinion on who they would like to have represent Onset. Let's get the word out and next week we'll vote on who will represent us."

At our next meeting we had a large attendance. A motion was made, seconded, and carried that Mr. Hanning should represent us at the Wharham Town Council meetings to get the ball rolling and get this debt under control.

I told them, "I accept this position."

Word got out and the Selectmen on the Wareham Council were really mad that I had been discussing this situation with the people in Onset. The Selectmen did not like me, and they tried to bury me all up.

It was tough going the first year. I started writing articles to put in the town paper, but the Selectmen would not put them in. They were looking them over one day when my friend, Dr. Charles Gleason, was in the office and overheard their conversation. He knew I was trying to get as much evidence as possible about three of the Selectmen, and he came to tell me, "Mr. Hanning, I don't expect you to take any action on this subject yet, but the other day I was in the Wareham Council office and I heard the men talking about the articles you wrote for the newspaper. One of them wanted to know what they should do with the articles. I don't know for sure which one spoke up, but I think it was the Chairman who said, "Throw them to H---in the waste basket."

I told him, "That is just the kind of information I have been hoping to hear, Dr. Gleason. It is some of the evidence I've been looking for."

He said, "Don't bring me into this."

Says I, "That is exactly what I shall do."

"Well," says he, "I shall tell the truth."

I told him, "That is exactly what I want you to do."

Wareham's council is made up of Selectmen and Officers elected each year. They have their meetings about every three weeks, unless a special meeting is called. They tend to take matters into their own hands, and run the town's affairs with little input from the public. About three months into attending these meetings, I felt it was time to get on the agenda for the next meeting, and I spoke with a friend who lived in Wareham asking him, "Charlie, will you please make a motion before we adjourn tonight, so I can talk at the next meeting. There are some issues I think we should discuss."

Charlie wanted to do this, because he knew we had to get the debt under control. The motion was made, but the Selectmen were very reluctant to even repeat it. After several moments of silence, someone in the audience spoke up and said, "I second the motion." The Selectmen looked at each other. You could tell they were discussing something. One of them finally said, "The motion is carried."

The time was coming when I had to lower the boom. I got all my ducks in a row and went to work. The first thing I found out at one of our meetings was that a whole bunch of people agreed with me, but I was told, "Nobody wants to rock the boat."

My response was, "I'm pretty familiar with a rocking boat so stay with me."

Before writing my speech, I carefully read the minutes of the last few meetings again to make sure I was being accurate in writing it. I also went to the Sheriff, got a warrant for three of the Selectmen, and had them indicted. The men were in shock. They were very frightened and had to give bonds.

The day arrived for the town meeting in Wareham, and we had a very crowded chamber. The Chairman of the Selectmen had a little bantam called John McSavary who was going to rip me all to pieces. He got up, made his speech, and sat down. I got up and told him, "I'm afraid I have hurt your feelings terribly by calling you a little bantam, for that makes you very conspicuous in town meetings. You flap your little wings. You would think you could stretch from pole to pole and span the oceans in your hands, but my little fellow you've got to be measured by your soul, for the mind is the stature of the man." Those attending the meeting cheered and laughed. He got up and tried to speak again. I told him, "Spit it right out," but he stammered and could not say a word.

I told those at the meeting, "The town of Wareham puts me in mind of a sailor that got tired of going to sea. When he got into New Orleans he thought he would go up the river to the farming area. He fell in with an old farmer on the Ohio River, and he was inquiring about what work he could get to do on a farm. The old fellow told him he thought he could get him a job with his neighbor. The sailor went over to talk to the old gentleman's neighbor and was hired. The next morning the owner of the farm yoked up his oxen and put them on the cart. Then he put old Cate, his mare on ahead of the oxen and drove them up to the door. He told the sailor to watch the team while he went in the house. The oxen started up the whiffletree and touched Cate's heels. (A whiffletree is also called whippletree or singletree. It is a heavy hook that pivots at the middle of a yoke to which heavy iron straps are attached to allow freedom of movement.)[37] Cate became very nervous and began to kick, fighting the oxen. They backed back, turned the yoke, and fetched Cate right in between them. She was kicking and the sailor did not know what to do. He ran into the house, told his boss the starboard ox was on the larboard (port) side and Cate was kicking up in the rigging. They were all going to Hades stern first, and that is the way our town is being run. We are kicking all the time and still the town is running into more debt." Those attending the meeting laughed so hard it was difficult getting the meeting under control and order restored.

"I am concerned about the way our Selectmen are going about this road building. It does not appear they have any clear-cut plans for the construction. It appears way too much money is being spent needlessly and something has to be done. Dirt is being moved from one spot to another and then has to be hauled back. Men are standing around doing nothing, sometimes for three hours at a time. The men are being paid for work they did with absolutely no records being kept. There does not appear to be any one person to oversee the entire operation of this project. If someone is hired to fill a position and quits, the next person seemingly is paid three to four times more than the first. The road is being built haphazardly and we cannot let it continue. We are already far too much in debt. This evening I propose we appoint a committee to look into the way the town is being run, and to see how the money has been laid out on the roads." There were ten people who volunteered to be on the committee, and I was appointed Chairman.

James H. Young said, "I make a motion to take the power from the Selectmen and appoint three road surveyors."

John McSavory, the little bantam said, "I second the motion."

Says I, "The motion is carried."

Now the selectmen have nothing to do with letting out contracts for the road. I asked, "Is there anyone who would like to make a motion to revoke the rule of electing three selectmen every year?" It was made and carried.

Another person spoke up and said, "I make a motion the selectmen should not have the handling of the town's money for making any contracts." That was carried too.

As I have stated, the town was twenty-seven thousand dollars in debt, and in eight years one of the Selectmen told me they saved enough money to pay off the debt. There was even enough money left in the treasury to start building a high school house.

About that time, I went out of the trolley business and I lost my wife. Mr. Porter, my partner, wanted to keep the real estate business, and we just dissolved our partnership. I settled everything up that needed to be done in Onset, packed up the things I wanted to take with me, sold my house and the things I was leaving behind, and tripped off to East Boston.

My wife, Roxana Weymouth Hanning, passed away January 11, 1906, in Wareham. (The following article was taken from the Wareham Courier Press, January 18, 1906, page 3)

Funeral services were held on Sunday at one o'clock for Mrs. Charles E. Hanning at her home on Twelfth Street. Mrs. Hanning was greatly beloved by all who knew her and her husband has the heartfelt sympathy of all who knew them.

Roxana and I lived in Onset for twenty-two years, and we both loved every minute of our life down there on the "Gateway to Cape Cod." It took almost a year after Roxana passed away for me to get everything in order so I could leave.

EAST BOSTON 1907-1917

I finally decided to retire so I could spend some time with my family. Through the years, I have not had much time to be with them because of my sea-faring life, but this was a perfect time to reunite with them. They were scattered throughout New England, and I decided to settle in East Boston. I was able to get a room in a boarding house, and I could travel from there.

Much has happened during the years. Although I was not physically with my girls much during their childhood, I most always knew what was going on. I often wished I could be closer to home, where I could be a part of their lives. This was the hardest part of making my livelihood sailing the oceans. I can never make up for all those things I've missed, but I feel really lucky to be able to spend time with them now.

I would like to tell you about my growing family after this past year of being with them.

Ellen, my oldest daughter, was twenty-two years old when she married Aaron Osgood Swett, September 15, 1874 in Boston, Massachusetts. They live in Newburyport, Massachusetts, where they made their home since at least 1880. There were no children born of this marriage.

Emma, my youngest daughter, was married twice. Her first marriage was to Almond Shepherd in 1873 when she was nineteen years old. Emma and Almond had three boys. Their names were George M., Charles H. Shepherd, and Ernest A. Shephard. (Note the difference in spelling the name.) I never met either George, nor Almond as they both passed away at a young age.

Emma's second marriage was to James A. Carr in 1893. Together they had two girls. Their names were Agnes and Janey Carr. The girls were in their early teens when they lost their mother in 1909, and to make matters worse their father had gone out west to prospect for gold. Fortunately their half-brother, Ernest Shephard, took care of them until they finished high school and could fend for themselves. I always enjoyed visiting with my grandchildren, learning about their past and the plans they had for their futures.

Emma Hanning Shepherd and Ernest Shepherd.

My two great-grandchildren were Almon and Sybil Shepherd. They were always on the move and talking up a storm. I will say they were quite well behaved youngsters. This past year has been one to treasure. During the next few years, I kept in close contact with my family and we always had good times when we were together. I think a great deal of them all.

I stayed in East Boston for one year. Then I decided to leave and go over to Somerville, just northwest of Boston, to stay with my wife's nephew, James A. Russ. I stayed there almost two years as we had such a good time when we were together.

When I returned to East Boston, I was able to get a room in a private house that I wanted to be in at 297 Meridian Street, East Boston, Massachusetts. I will say I had another sick spell while I was with this family, but I had the best of care from everybody.

Dr. Campbell, my physician, did everything that could be done and he pulled me through. I have had very good health up to my present writing, and now I am in my eighty-second year with a wonderful family I think of often. I moved into my home exactly one year ago today. Incidentally, my daughter Ellen will be fifty-nine years old in several weeks on August 11, 1911.

I started writing about the many adventures I have had throughout my life's journey back in 1908, shortly after I returned from the first visit I had with my children. I was then almost seventy-nine years old, and here we are three years later and I'm still writing. Aging is not something we can control, but I'm going to try to be as active as possible. I still go back to Onset every now and then to visit my friends, and when they come to Boston, we try to get together. My Boston friends and I get together for lunch at least once a month, and then I have this pleasant family I live with that I like very much. The great problem with them is they pet me too much. I feel just as much at home here as I would in my own home. I have every privilege that a boarder can have, and I have never heard or felt any disagreeable thing the whole time that I have been here.

In all my adventures I have found friends and good ones too. I cannot say that I was even abused when I was a prisoner for the Confederates did everything they could for me.

Reflecting back on my life as I have been writing about it, I find that if you know a trade you want to follow, work hard at mastering it, stand up for what you know is right, be kind and thoughtful to those around you, have faith, and follow your dreams, anyone can succeed. My life has been an amazing journey.

(Charles Elisha Hanning was born May 25, 1830, and died January 8, 1917, at the Soldier's Home in Chelsea, Massachusetts, just four months shy of his eighty-seventh birthday. He was buried in the Belleville Cemetery in Newburyport, Essex, Massachusetts.)

The following article was taken from the Wareham Courier Press, January 11, 1917. Page number not listed.

William M. Griffin received word late last evening of the death of Captain Charles Elisha Hanning at East Boston, where he has made his home for the past few years. He was over 80, but did not look near that, and had enjoyed good health. About a month ago he visited Mr. and Mrs. Griffin. He resided here many years and when the horse car line was the only means of travel between Onset Junction and Onset, he drove a barge. Everybody knew Captain Hanning. He was always courteous, kind and ready to do a kindness, and when his barge or carriage was free from passengers, every child that could pile in was given a ride.

BIBLIOGRAPHY

1. Aroostook War, 1839, Wikipedia.org

2. New World Dictionary, Simon and Schuster, 1986, weather boards

3. Mexican American War, 1846-47, Wikipedia.org

4. Wikipedia, Glossary of nautical terms, stores

5. en.wikipedia.org. Istanbul

6. Vinow.com/general-usvi/geography, St. Thomas Island

7. New World Dictionary, Simon and Schuster, 1986, spiles

8. Glossary of nautical terms-wikipedia, hawser

9. Glossary of nautical terms-wikipedia, chocks

10. New World Dictionary, Simon and Schuster, 1986, werewolf

11. en.wikipedia.org/wiki/Panama-Canal-Railroad

12. en.wikipedia.org/wiki/Ambon-Island, ambonia wood

13. Wikipedia.org/wiki/glossary nautical terms, mizzenmast

14. Wikipedia.org/wiki/glossary nautical terms, terms used by captains

15. en.wikipedia.org/wiki/Cay-Sal-Bank

16. en.wikipedia.org/wiki/San-Juan-River, Lake Nicaragua

17. en.wikipedia.org/wiki/William-Walker-filibuster

18. en.wikipedia.org/railroad-tie, sleeper

19. New World Dictionary, Simon and Schuster, 1986, marlinspike

20. New World Dictionary, Simon and Schuster, 1986 log flume

21. New World Dictionary, Simon and Schuster, 1986, drum head court martial

22. en.wikipedia.org/wiki/Madiu Indians

23. en. wikipedia.org/wiki/Jakarta-Batavia

24. Google-tatagla wood/hardwood tree found in the Philippines Islands

25. en.wikipedia.org/wiki/Sunda Strait

26. en.wikipedia.org/wiki/Anyer, Anger town in Banten

27. en.wikipedia.org/wiki/Banka-Belitung-Islands

28. en.wikipedia.org/wiki/Sittwe, Akyab, Burma now Myanmar

29. en.wikipedia.org/wiki/Parole-camp

30. en.wikipedia.org/wiki/Battle-of-Culpepper-Court-House

31. New World Dictionary, Simon and Schuster, 1986, sutler

32. New World Dictionary, Simon and Schuster, silver nitrate

33. en.wikipedia.org/wiki/4th-Maine-Volunteer-Infantry-R

34. en.wikipedia.org/wiki/Boston-Navy-Yard

35. dictionary reference.com/browse/keeper

36. hollyhurstcottageinn.com/onsethistory.htm

37. New World Dictionary, Simon and Schuster, 1986, whiffletree

LIFE

OF

Charles

Elisha

Hanning.

—

Autobiography.

Written at age of 84 years.

— 1916 —

J.H. CLINE

Hand calligraphy cover of the original manuscript by J.H. Cline.

Charles Elisha Hanning
                        Ward 1. East Boston Mass.
297 Meridian St. East Boston Mass.
Born in Portland Maine 25 day of may 1830.
Enlisted in 4 Maine Co. E. Regiment April 29 1861.
Discharged July 19. 1864. at Rockland Maine
Age 83 years and 4 months.
Resident 297 Meridian St. East Boston Mass.

                        Charles Elisha Hanning.

A seth of the life of Charles E Hanning
written by himself who is almost 79 years
old, I was born in Portland Maine 25 day
of may 1830. My mother went to old Town
Maine, when I was three months old and
my father went to sea as shipmaster,
and he accumalated quite a fortune for them
days, and he left the sea and went in
lumbering and real estate, and lost all
that he had and became very poor, and
it was about the time I should have gone
to school, in them days they did not
have free schools, and my father could
not afford to send me to school, so when
I got large enough to work I done every
thing could, when I was ten years old
I worked and bought me the first pair
of books I ever had, I tell you that I
was a proud boy, when I got any money
I would give it to my mother, for I
loved her and I love to think of her,
I left home when I was very young

and went to sea, I ran away when I was thirteen years old and I was gone 7 years, and my folks did not know me when they saw me I had a full beard and looked several years older than I was, I was with one man all the time, he was the best man that ever lived, his name was Capt. Everett Chase, and he was a Father to me he was Master of a topsail schooner called the north branch and I was with him two years in her, and then he had a new squarerigged brig for him she was about three hundred tons, she was called John Gillipin and was a fine vessell after he got her his wife went with us and she was a lovely woman, they bought books for me and learnt me and took all the pains that could be taken with me, and the Capt. learnt me novagation and all the comercial business, he went mostly on forgine voyages several times to Europe. and one voyage was around Cape Horn on a trading voyage, we went to masagegland mexico, and from there we went to Santiago California it was in

April 1848, we left there the last of April
for Bombay in ballast and there we loaded
for Harvd France with cotton, my 17 birthday
was on the Pacific Ocean, we did not hear of
gold being found in California sintill we got
to France, we went from Harvre to St Thomas
Danish W. I. and from there we whent to Vera cruz
Mexico, and from there to Boston and the Capt.
whent home and I whent Master, I was then
in my 20th year, and the owners thought I
was too young to go master, so they got an
old Captian to go Mate with me, and I
had all the trouble I wanted and if I had
let him had his way he would have
lost the vessele, he would not do any thing
that I told him to do, he told the second
Officer and the crew that I was a baby Capt.
and had not got my dry pers off yet, and the
second Officer told me what he said, I
called him aft and I read the riot act to
him I asked him what he meant he said
he meant just what he said, I told him
to his room, and he said he had command

and would do as he pleased, and I said if he gave me any of his impudence that I would put the irons on him, he went off off duty I took the second Officer for first mate, and was off duty three days, and he came to me and said he would do as I told him. if I would put him on duty, and he done quite well for some time, when I got off Galavastone the weather looked bad the wind was too the easteard and it looked like a bad storm I came up alongside of a morfidate brig, and the Capt. hailed me and wanted to know if I was going in to Galavastone, and before I could speak the mate said no I told him to shut up his head, and I told the Captian that I was going in and I went in, the Capt. kept out and he was blown down in the Gulf and was blown all to peices, and it was three weeks before he got back, we was both bound for Galavastone. I went in over both bars and up the river, and let go my big anchor she swung around and I let

go my other anchor and I run my hossers to
some pilles ashore and made fast with the
bite and fetched the other end on the
starboard side and made fast and laid
all night it was an oful gale I was laying
close to the shore, but I did not go ashore
the next day it blew so hard and there was
eight vessels lost on the outter and inner bar
in the storm but I was all right, and the
third day I hauled in and commenced to
discharge. I let my Mate go and he worked
his way up to New Orleans in a small
schooner, and he wrote the owners an oful
letter that they never would see the vessel
again, he called me everything but a white
man, but he never went home again, I
think it was well for him that he never did
I loaded for New York and when I got in
New York I wrote to the agent and he came
on to New York with the idea of turning
me out, when he got there I showed him
the bills and a letter that the shipper gave
me, and I said I suppose you got a letter

from the old Mate and he said that he
had but he did not tell me what he said
I told him he could put another Capt, in
her if he wanted to and he said I had
better go in he said he was satisfied
with me and I got a chater to go back to
the same port and get a chargo for Boston
and I sent down east and got another Mate
that I knew he was a good fellow and I had
a good time that voyage and got back to Boston
and the owners sold the brig and they built
me a Barque that summer I went down
east and worked on her and they sold her
before she was launched, and I went to the
West Indies that winter, and the next summer
they built me a larger barque, and I went
to New Orleans and from there I went to
Havra France and from there I went to
Rigino Brijial and from there to New York
and we sold her and the owners had another
larger one almost finished and I took her
and went to New Orleans with a boad of
brick and hay, and from there I went to

Mantanases West Indies, and back to New Orleans
and I loaded there with cotton for New York
and there I loaded with lumber General
cargo for Shagnes in the isthmus of Panamaha
that was when they was building the railroad
and I went from there to Verycruge - Mexico
I went down the coast about 20 miles and
loaded with logwood and lingivity for Hava
Hrancel and the port of Bordul and I
loaded there for Boston and I left her to take
a Ship for Caloa Preul and from there I
went to Chicey Islands and loaded with
Geneou for Hapdlen roads, I went home
and took a barque that was building for me
she was all ready and I went to Havanaha
Cuba and back to New York and sold her
and I sold out and went to California.
I was married when I was 22 and it was a
very unhappy thing for me, and I broke up
and went away and I was gone five years.
When I went away I left two children and left money
to take care of them, I was at sea part of the
time that I was gone I went as an Officer

on the Pacific steamers that run to Panama
and after I left them, I went up in the mountains
and went to mining, but my luck was poor
and I worked at carpentering a while and I went
into butcering I had a meat market on the
north fork of the feather river, but I got a
sever cold driving cattle over the mountains,
and it cost me two thousand one hundred dollars
before I got so I could do anything, after I got
able I went further up the river and started
in the same business and I acculamated money
and my health was poor and I went down to
Frisco, I was up in the mountains all most
two years, and my health was so poor that the
Dr, advised me to go across the Pacific Ocean
and I found there was only one vessell in Port
that was going across and that one was going to
Honghong China, and he wanted a second
Officer but he would not take a passanger
so I shipped second mate and he was a brute
but I was full a match for him, we went
from Honghong to Batavia we went down
through the Philipine Islands, and we loaded

for Sansacranfico California from I shipped as
mate of a ship and went to Mellburne Australia
and from there we went to Anger Point in the
straits of Gasper in the Indian Ocean and from
there we went to Garver head and from there to
Sinnapaw for orders and was ordered to Accababe
and we could not get a freight so we went to
Calluctta india and got a freight for Boston,
While I was in Calluctta, I fell in with one of
the most remarkable men I ever saw, he was
a Buddhist Priest of Persia, he knew the most
of any man I ever talked with, he told me
more about the United States than I knew
myself, and I learned more the two months
that I was aquainted with him than in all
my life previous to that, he told me of the
Planets and the different religions and how city
was built and about the nations of the world
he said the Americans was the brightest people
because they was the most Western Nation on
the earth. He used to come aboard of the ship
every day but Sunday and take dinner
with me, and we would talk about everything

for he could talk seven different languges, he could talk the English language just as fulently as I could and as plain, he said I did not know what you folks meant; he said that the American people had everything to make them happy, we had a good Government only we held slaves and that was not right; but that would be overcome by the greatminds then the people would be free, and prousprous that we had large hearts and christian spirits always ready to respond to those that was in need he told me my nationathty from my birth and my past life he told me the minute and the hour that I was born. I liked the man and I should liked to have seen him again, that was fifty one years ago, and he was quite an old man then: I got back to Boston and whent to Belfast Maine where my Children was and took care of them. I got a Divorce from my wife, and when the civilewar broke out I enlisted in Co E, fourth Maine regment and I served 3 years and 3 months, I was wounded twice

the first time I was taken a Prisoner and carried
to Leibey prison in Richmond I was Paroled and
sent to Annapolis Maryland, but in all my
adventures I found friends and good ones too, I
could not say that I was abused when I was
a prisoner the Confederts done everything they
could for me, I had my right shoulder
dislacated they did everything that could be done
for me they set it and did it well.

I was a praloed prisnor in Annapolis in Maryland I was there from the last of January then I was exchanged and went back to my regiment at Falmoulth then the army moved there days after I returned on the second vedersburge battle and my regiment was engaged at Chansovill and the third day our army fell back across the Rsaphanick river and we went in the Merion army phent in the old gwaters then the army under general Hocker moved on to Gettesburge where it had there days fighting but I was sent to Washington with the typhord fever and was very sick for two montts and then I was sent fort Shyler N.Y. to the convenselent Hospital.

From there the 3 day of July 1863 I got
a furlog for thirty days to go home to
Belfast Maine. to see and look after
my children two girls 7 and nine years of
age. when my furlough was up I
went back to my regiment which
was laying at white sulpher springs Va.
next day after I got to my regiment
the army mooved on the Confederts
and we had a fight at Kellysford on
the Rapadanna river there we took a
squad of refels about 400 in number
and drove the rebls out of their winter
quaters at brandy station whare we had
a fight and tht was in November 1863 and
we when in the Union army whent into the
rebels winter quaters for the Union winter
quaters and we laid there all tht winter
with the exception of our corps
recortening once third corps

and on the 4 day of May 1864 General Grant
the commanded the army of Pontevac
gave orders to be to move at 12 Oclock that
night and it was 10 Oclock when we got
the orders I had just came in of a picket
and had just turned in for the night the
Captin of my company which I was ordely
Sargent give me orders to fall in the
Company and I did and he the Capt- gave us orders
to be Ready march at 12 Oclock that night
with 8 days rations five days in the
haversack and three in napsack with
40 rounds of catriges in our catrige box
and we started at the hour of 12 midnight
and we marched 33 miles, with the exeption of
of 30 minuts to get breckfast in the morning
after we crossed the Rappadan and we never
made another halt untill we gained our
position at Chancellorville and our regment
beverwached one year to a day after the

second Fedsburge fight - thd was the 4 day
of May 1864 and we arrived there at 2 P.M.
and the the 5-day we went to recortening to
find the enemy and we did not hunt long
before we found them and we was engaged at
3 Oclock in battle whare we lost heavely and
one thing I would say in the engagement - I
had the bottom of my haversack shot
out and I lost all the balance of my five day
rations and we laid on our arms all night
and the next morning, we mad a charge, and
took about one begrade and a half of reble
prisoners and on the charge just as I was
stepping up off the bank road there was
a bullet struck me in the forehead
whet through my forehead just over the
right eye, where it took a glanceing direction
whet around my skull just over my right
ear and lodged in the back part of my
skull.

and I was insensible when my old bregade
Commander J. H. Hobert Ward came up
and he see me and knew who I was & he told
his ordely to get me on his horse and take me
to the rear to the hospital & in about half an
hour the rebles had the ground where I lay,
& I was not conscious of any thing for 14 days
but I could not remember any thing for that
peroid of time, I was sent to Washington
and there I came to myself particulay, I
sent to Meridian hill hospital and there
I stayed 2 days but I had gained concenssion
and from there I was sent to Philidelpha
McClellan hospital and 21 days after I was
wounded the Drs dressed my wound and
trappaned it, the Drs wanted to give me
ether and I would not take it, so they put
me in a barbers chair and the wound was
dressed 21 after I was wounded and when
the Dr put silver over the wound I fainted
twice.

and the third time just came to conchiness
and the old Dr. that had charge said if he
faints again he wont come out of it. I just
heard enough of what he said to say I haint
a going to. and they dressed it and put me on
my cot, and the ward master said that I laid
3 days without saying anything. and they gave me
stemults and what they could get into me and
the fourth day they brought me some beef
tea had about ½ pint and a glass tube I
consumed the beef tea and called for more
which was brought. they gave me all that I
asked for untill I could take solid food
and I began to gain strength untill I
recovered. And my enrolement was out
and I wanted to go home and I supposed I
was going down to Philidelpha to get
transportation home and they sent me to
Washington instead to the despertution
camp at Arlington Va.

So I could not find out what to do and they told me about a woman that would get me trasportation and I whent to see her, and she had an Officer and she gave me pretty short answer and I turned abruptly and whent off when I got back to the camp the orderly there had detailed me to build a fence, and I told him to go to whare they did not rake up fire over night, and I whent to see General Hainshalman. and I told him who I was he said all right Ill see to that he told his ordely to go get his Horse and his own and I supposed he was going off som whare but when the orderly came up he gave me a note and told me to get on that horse and go to Whasington which was 7 miles, there I could get trasportation I thanked him very kindely and left and got my trasportation there I fell in with one of General Wards Aide he told me General Ward was in Washington and I whent to see him and he told me that when he told his ordely to take me back to the Hospital he never expected to see me again.

He told me that the fourth Maine regment
was at the depo going home that night and I
went down to the depo and found it. I went
to Boltimore and there I left the regement
and went on my own hook, as I had transportation
when I got to N.Y. I found the regement there
so I kept on in a different train from N.Y.
to Boston. and next morning I got at the Boston
main depo I found my regement there. But
I kept on and went to Agusta Maine. and I
took the stage there and went to Belfast accross
the country 40 miles. and I went to my old
bording truse that was about 2 A.M. and
they had seen paper whare I was dead and they
was suprised to me resuceded as they suppos
on the 19 of July 1864 I was mustered out to
service and in Sept. I got a chance in the navy
yard at latarstown to work at $4.00 per day
I worked about 15 months and then my old agent
wanted me to go to Leiverpool England and get a
ship I was in her about one and a half years I
was married about 4 months after I went in
the navy yard and when I left the ship I had
been in her about 16 months. She was sailing
under an English register I did not
like it

So I got my old position in the Navey yard my
wife and children joined me in Charaston and we
went to keeping house two daughters by my first wife
which lived with us one was 7 and the other 10 when
they came to live with us and my wife was very fond
of them, and they thought a great deal of her, she
did not have any children of her own, but every
body that did not know that they where not her
children thought they was, they looked so much
like her, I worked in the navey yard about 3 years
then I went to Phildelphia and looked after the
repairing and overhaling of a barque for my
brotherinlaw the barque was called the General W. J.
Sherman, when I put the gang of men on her
to do the work they was going to tear her all
to peices, then I told them what I wanted done
I was putting a sugar deck on her and they
said they wanted to tear out certain work
I told them to do just as I told them then
they said they would not do any thing

and I told them it was all right—I told the
agent to report her to sail for Boston with a
load of coal, I was going to Port Richmond
to load with coal for Boston, and the boss
carpenter came to see me and wanted to know
what the trouble was, I told him they would not
do as I ordered them to, so he told me to wait
he told the men if they would not do as I
wanted them to to leave he would not employ
them, they came back I told them they could
go to work at noon I would not allow them
any there for the forenoon, and they reported to
the boss and he told them ttd would be all
right—they could not get any there not untill noon
so at 1 Oclock they went to work two of them
worked about 1/2 and hour went of thy was
gone about one and a half hours and came
back for to go to work I told them they could
pick up their tools and go ashore I did not
want men of ttd style I wanted men to keep on
their work

and they all five left, and I was going to Port
Richmond and the boss come down and put
on some men they worked study untill they got
the carpenter work all done, then the caukers
came on and they undertook to play the same
trick they thought I could not come without
the deck being caulked, there where six of them
they worked about 1/2 an hour, they then went away
and stayed about one hour, when they came back
I told them to pick up their tools and get ashore
and they did I threw the okume out on the warfth
went to the office to settle with the carpenter
she wanted to know what the trouble was, I told
to him after they had worked 1/2 an hour they all
went ashore and was gone about one hour, and
when they came back I told them to go ashore
and stay and they wanted to know how I was
going to get along without caulking the deck,
I told them that was none of their business
to get ashore or I would help them to

and they went ashore. I went up to the office to settle and the boss he thought I was having a good deal of trouble I told him I thought so too for I wanted men to work I did not want them loafing so we let them go, and sent me some more men, they did first rate and finished the work up, and when I went to settle with them he had me charged with several day's work that I hadent had I told him I would not pay no such bill as that, I showed my account of the work and material and I could prove that so he settled with me at my account, and I loaded the vessel with general merdensise and went to Savannah Georgia and there I loaded with railroad tie's for New York, then my brotherinlaw took the vessel and I came home to Charlstown, and I mooved from Charlstown to E. B. and kept a boarding hous for one and a half years on Meridian St.

and there I got burned out the big fire in 1870
and I lost everything, fortunately I was insured, then
I whent to Boston and kept a boarding house there
for a year and a half, and was very fortunate
there I sold out at a good fireman, and whent
in to the Groarice business in Malden but
my business was not so fortunate and I sold out
and whent in the real estate business, and was
quite successful the first year then panic times
came on and I lost about 1800 dollars, and had
to give the business up, then I whent in the
grocery business again for a short time, and
done quite well, I sold out and whent in the
ship carpenter business carried ttd on for
about 3 years my wife was decling in health,
and I whent down to Onsets bay, on the old
Conlony road Cape Cod, and I built me a house
and mooved down there and I lived there 23 years,
and I whent into business in teaming and livery
business, and baggage business they where

building a horse railroad from East Warham
to Onset they wanted me to take stock in the road
and become a director and boss carpenter, and I
took one share with the understanding that I would
take 3 or 4 more if everything was satisfactory, and
they had their meeting to elect officers and they
engored me never let me know any thing about
it, and they tried to keep it from me, but I
found out what they had done, and I paid
8.50.00 on the share I had bought, — one
hundred dollars a share, after they had got
the business all ready to start the road in
the mean time the Presdient got me to figure
up how much lumber it would take and
how many sleepers and then they engored me
all together, when I found it out I read the
riot act to the Presdient, and I told them I would
not have any thing more to do with them. I told him
that he had lied to me and I was done with
him, he saide there had been a mistake
                                        made

I told him there was no mistake made there was a lie made, and he said he took me for a different kind of a man, I told him I supposed he took me for a fool, but I took him for a truthful man, now says I you found out that I am not a fool and I have found out you are a notorious liar, and he started and went across the street then came back, and said it was a mistake and did not want our friendship broke up, he would call another meeting and have the former meeting annuled, this was Saturday and he would call the meeting the next Monday night, Sunday he and I went over the road talked about affairs concerning the road, and Monday we was consulting each other, and Monday night passed I did not get any notice Tuesday I saw the President the President name was Thomas B. Griffice and he did not say any thing to me Tuesday about what they had done, and I got a letter from E. B. they wanted me to come up;

to take charge on Ship work. So Wedensday I packed
up my things, and came up to E. B. my wife was with
me, when we was going up I was in the coach with
the Presdient and one of the directors and the Presdien
wanted to make some tolk with me, about some work
he had on his house, I told him he could get any
one to do it he wanted to as I did not want any of
his work and he could go where they did not rake up
fire over night. and my wife asked me who the man
was I talked the way to I told her it was old Griffie
she did not know him by sight. and they did not say
any thing more to me, when I got up to the depo, they
sent the chairman of the selectman to enquire
where I was going, I told them I was going crazy I
guess, and he got abroad the cars with me and
whent to tremont about 7 miles, he did not find
out any thing my wife and I came to Boston, and
that was in April I stayed untill July, then I
whent down to Onset and stayed over the 4 in the
mean time while I was there I sold my share

that I paid $.50.00 for for $.10.00 the man paid
the balance and got his share for $.60.00. I told him
now I have $.10.00 for my share and you will never
receive quarter of the $.10.00 let alone the other $.50.00
and the first year they got 2 1/2 per cent and there
was not a stock holder after the first year that
ever got a dollar, I stayed in E.B. one year when I
went back I had made $.600.00 clear of all expences,
When the first year that the horse cars run there was
a man put a choach on with 2 horses, and the horse
cars run him of in 40 days, so the next spring
when I went back to Onset I told a friend of mine
that was driving their first car, that I would advance
him seven hundred dollars to buy a span of horses
and a coach to run in opposition to the horse railroad
and I would help him, and he would not do it, so
I bought my horses and the coach I started it
myself, and the first time I went to the depo
I carried 9 passangers the horse cars did not get any
when I came down from the depo I brought 17
passangers,

td was on Saturday and td night I got $3.00 to carry a party home from a dance, and the next morning I went to the depo with my team and got a full load of passangers down, they was hanging on the coach every whare, and I got eleven trunks tht I had to go back after, the horse cars got 4 trunks, the Presdient Griffice he was rageing and said thay drove the orther fellow off in 40 days and thay would drive me in 2 days, my friend tht I offered to fit up, with a team tht was driving their first car told him he was mistaken, he said do you know anything about Hanning he said nothing more than he had got aquainted with him there, he told him I have been talking with a man tht has known him all his life, and he said you can defend tht he has come to stay with you, and the Presdient went to the old lonely officials wanted him to drive me away from the depo and the officials told them in their power, tht the depo was a publice place for everybody, thay wanted to know if thay could not stop me from collecting baggage, thay told him thy could stop me from soliciteing

but if any one wanted me to carry their baggage,
they could not stop me, they went to the depo
master and he said he would not deliver it to
me they had brought him, so I took my checks
and went right into the baggage room, and
went to taking the trunks out, and he forbid
me from taking them, then I went for him he
went to the office and locked himself in, and
he told me that he would report me to the road,
for making trouble, I got my trunks and gave
the checks to the freight agent he was friendly,
and I wrote a letter to the Superintendent stating
what the agent done, and when I mail'd the letter
I told the agent that he could pack his
grip for his service would not be needed
any longer, he said he guessed I would
find out that I could not come there any
more, next morning I met the agent there at
the depo, I did not say any thing to him at
first, says I there is of the horse railroad
men and the freight agent, there is my letter
I wrote to you I can prove every word of it,
and there is the men that heard what was said

now if you will please read the letter or I will
read it for you, said he could read it very plain
so he read it right before the depo master, and
a lot of folks and passangers was standing around
on the platform, and the depo master whent to
mak an evasise answer, he asked him what
he had to say to that, then he told I want
you to answer, well yes he said it was just
as I had stated, then he wanted it stated
what the President of the horse car road
said, and the railroad agent said that was
none of his business, he said what
authority had you, to refuse delivering
them trunks when the checks was presented
he said that major Goffice President of the
horse railroad told him not too, he said
do you want this company sued for damages,
says he you give me up the keys of the depo
he says does that mean my discharge yes he
said it does immediately you have nothing
more to say here, he told the freight
agent, to take the keys and engage a man
for a freight agent, which there was one

standing right on the platform, the President
of the horse railroad, he wanted to make some talk
with the agent, he told him he had no time whent
off and left him standing there, with his heart
almost broken. and I took my trunks and
delivered them, with cheers by the passengers
railroad
and men at the depo, then the President of the horsecar got
his men to do everything they could to bother me
this friend of mine that was driving their first
car he told me and I just told them to stop
their music right away and they did, and then
they got a worthless chaether to come and bother
me, he whent to meddling with my passangers
and I sot him up in shoe buisness I boted
him about 3 hundred feet every time he would
try to get up I set him up in the shoe buisness
and he prosecuted me for assualt and it they
fined me $10 dollars and I foolishly appealed
and it cost me about 85 dollars, in all, but
I got rid of him and the agent he had bought
a peice of land alongside the railroad
for the railrade and had got a deed of it, and
the man that sold it to him had my claim

he had sold it to other parties and deeded it to them, and had left the state. But the one he sold it to had given him back a mortgage for $1,150.00 payable in one year and I found out all the circumstances, when the mortage came due a lady told me she had to pay 25 per cent to get the money to pay the mortgage, I told her would she would not have to she said she did not know where she could get it unless she got it from me, I told her she could I said I would settle it too I said you let me know when he comes, and I will settle with him he waited untill about 1/2 past 8 Oclock Saturday night I was waiting for him and the Lady came to my house to let me know in the mean time I had got out a warrent for him, his name was Martin, and I had spoken to a constable to be ready to serve the warrent, and when I went in to the notary publics Mr James. H. Young, Martin was there very much suprised to see me and I told him I had come to settle up the mortage and also for a load of wood he stole from me

and he said he did not recolect that I said
I know you dont, then I told him what I had
done, now I have concluded to give you $150.00
for the mortgage if you got it here I want it
if you dont come to my terms, you will stay
in the lock up untill Monday morning. he wanted
to know what he had done I told him that he
sold property that did not belong to him and
that was a state prison offence, he said he
had paid Mrs Hammond for the land says
I how did you pay her, he told her that
he got 20 for the land you gave her 15 dollars
I said did not the railroad pay 35 dollars
for the land you said you only got 20 $ for it
now I said you got $20.00 and she got $15.00
now I said what have you got to say to that
and he said he forgot I said dont you lie
to me, now I said I have no more time to
fool with you so you can come to my terms
or go to the lock up, and he began to cry and
Mrs Hammond called me into another room said
we better give him one hundred dollars I
said no I wont finaly we gave him $75.00

and I told him to get out of the place as quick as he could for if it was not for his wife and children I would have him arrested anyway, and now I said you are liable to be arrested by the old Conoly road for fraud, and he left has never been seen since, I saw Mr Taylor the division agent that bought the land of Martin for the railroad, and I told him just how he was fixed he wanted to know if I was sure I said yes I am for I done the business for Mrs Hammond I looked the records over, before I paid the Mortage off, and I found that her deed had been recorded before Martin gave him a deed, Well he said what can I do I told him you can get extidition papers and fecth him back to Mass. and put him in state prison, but he said would not give him a title to the land. so I told I can fix it for you I told him how I would do and so he said if you will do it I will make it all right, so I got Mrs Hammond to make another deed to the old Conoly railroad and she signed it and I gave it to him and he wanted to know what my bill was, I told

him that it would be one dollar and seventy five
cents a dollar for making out the deed and 75 cts for
recording, well he said what have I got to pay you
I told make that right here at the depo so he
gave me two stands at the depo and gave the
depo master orders to keep it for me, and I got
the deed recorded and gave it to the agent and I
was not troubled any more, and it almost broke
the railroad's President heart again, and every
year the stockholders wanted to know what their
divedends was going to be, he would tell them
to go to Hanning and get their divedends, for they
pataronised him instead of the railroad, they
run the railroad about 14 years and it cost
$22 000.00 and they sold it for fourteen
hundred with 2 lots of land and Hanning
at that time owned 5 houses, and several
lots of land in Onset and 20 acers of
between Onset and East Wharham, which he
sold the 20 acers afterwards for $1300.00 dollars
and when he sold it, it only cost him $2.00
he had managed it so that he had got
enough of it to pay the priciple and interest

and tapes and all the labour he done on it, so
ttd it was just the same though he had bought
t fo 8.2.00 and ttd peice of land has paid
him about $940.00 and now holds a mortagge
in it for $.1100.50. Now I will go back to town
affairs, they where stealing the selectmen and offeers
of the Town where stealing so ttd the Town
was $.27000.00 in debt, and I whent after
them and the first year they buried me all
up, and the next year I wrote several articuals
to put in the town want, and setelectmen
would not put them, because it was old
Hannings articuals, they was looking over
one day before town meeting and one of the
selectmen wanted to know what they was
going to do witt them, they all spoke up and
said throw them to Hell in the waist basket.
Dr Charles Gleason was in the Office and
heard what they said, and he told me did not
suppose I was going to take any action but I
was getting evedeence and he told me what
they said, and the district attorney told
me ttd was just what he wanted

and I told Dr Gleason that was just what
I was hunting for, he says dont bring me into
it says I that is just what I shall do, well says
he I shall tell the truth, and I got out a warrent
for all three selectmen I had them indited
and they had to give bonds and they was pretty
scared, we had the town meeting in about
3 weeks after they was indited and the chairman
of the selectmen had a little bantam called
J. Mack Savary, he was going to rip me
all to pieces, he got up and made his speech
and when he sat down, I got up and it hurt
his feelings terrible to call him a little
bantam, that makes himself very
conspicuous in town meeting he flopped
his little wings and you would think he
would strech from pole to pole and span
the Oceans in his hands but the little
fellow has got to be masured by his soul
for the mind is the stature of the man,
They cheered and laughed, he got up and
tried to speak, I told him to spit
it right out, he stammered and could not sa

& them that the town of Wareham put me in mind
of a sailor that got tired of going to sea, when he got
in to New orleans thought he would go up the river to
farming and he fell in with an old farmer on the
Ohio and he was inquiring about what he could get to
do on the farm the old fellow told him he thought
he could get him a Job if he would go up to Ohio
said he thought he had a neighbour that would give
him a Job. so he went to work for this man and the
next morning he yoked up his oxen and put them
on the cart and he put old Kate on ahead of them
his Mare, and drove up to the door told the fellow
to watch the team while he went in the house,
the oxen started up the whiffel tree touched Kates
heels she was neverous, and began to kick sprinkling
the oxen, they backed back, and turned the yoke
fetched her right in between them, she was kicking
and the sailor did not know what to do, he ran in the
house told the man that starbord ox was on the
larboard side and Kate was kicking up in
the rigging they was all going to haylies stern
first, and that is the way our town is running
we are kicking all the time and still the town

is running in debt, they laughed so it was hard
work to restore order, then I proposed to appoint-
a committe for to look in the way the town had
been running and to see how the money had been
laid out on the roads, they appointed me,
chairman of the committe, and James H. Young
and John McSavery and I made a motion to take
the power from the Selectmen and appoint three
road suvaryes the motion was carried, and the
selectmen had nothing to do with letting out-
contracts for the town, and I mad a motion to
revoke the rules of the town to elect our selectmen
every year all three of them, and it was carried, I
made a motion the selectmen, should not have
the handling of the town's money for making any
contracts and it was carried, At the time the
town was $. 27000.00 in debt- and in eight years
from that time one of the selectmen told me
that they had money enough in the treasury
to pay off the debt- and they took the money
to build a high school house, about that time
I went out of business and I lost my wife and
sold out every thing and went to Boston

I petured and I united with my grandchildren that lived in Vermont. I had 4 Grandchildren two boys and two girls, and one daughter-a living and two great-grandchildren one a boy and one a girl, that I have visited and I think a great deal of them, my daughter now living at present time is all most 59 years old in August 1911 she will be 59 years old, about a year after I came to E.B. I had a very sick spell I was lodging at the time with a private house I had the best of care from everybody Dr Campbell my pyshician, done everything for that could be done and pulled me through then up to the present writing I have had very good health and now I am in my 82 year boarding on Meridian St-297 E.B. with a very pleasant family and I like very much the great trouble is they pet me too much I feel just as much at home as I would in my own house have every privlege that a boarder can have, lived at the present place about 10 months I have never heard or felt any disagreable thing the whole time that I have been there,

written by myself who is almost 79 years old
I was born in Portland Maine 25 day of May
1830. My Mother went to oldtown Maine with
me when I was 3 months old, my Father went to
sea as shipmaster in a ship that was built for
him the year before, but he's family had lived
in oldtown several years, on a farm so when he
had a ship built in Portland Mother went there to
stay with her folks so she could be with Father
and when he got ready to sail she had to stay
there untill I arrived, they had no steamers
running from Portland to Bangor and she had to
go to Bangor in a sailing vessel, when I was 3
months old and I suppose that was why I was a
sailor, my Father retired from forgine
voyages when I was about 2 1/2 years old, and as
stated before lost his property and had to go
to sea again, but he went coasting and when
I was in my ninth year the United States and
England had trouble about the boundry line
and there was a war cloud arose and Maine
sent a force of volunteers along the boundery
line between Main and New Brunswick

and my Father he done teaming for the govenment
and when they settled it and the troops returned
I coaxed him to let me go with him to drive
one of the teams for to bring the suplies back to
Bangor and everywhare we stoped to every
public house the soliders and the woman folks
went crazy over me, Father could not do anything
would not allow him any control over me, and
he told me when he got me home he would
settle with me; but he never did, we was gone
2 and a half days and ete first night whare
we stopped they made me a uniform and the
soldiders made a swoard for me and the girls
mad Scarbord they put appletts on my
shoulders I was a full fledged Captian
and the soldiers that saw me after that
always called me the young Captian,
and when I got back home one of the
Sargeents let me have his horse to ride
into the villiage, and I rode along side of
the general and the folks at ete public
house went wild, Father told me I better
go home and see my Mother, they sent for

about a mile when she saw me in uniform
she wanted to know what they had been doing
to the child she took me up in her arms and
sat down, I told her Mama you ought not
make a baby of me for I was captain then
& went home with her and everybody in the
place was running to see me, one woman
told Mother she would give her farm with
a sawmill on it for me, my sisters was
jelous of me and would make fun of me for
being a soldier we went out in the woods
and I climbed a tree when I was up in the
tree they went to cutting it down to scare me
when they got it almost ready to fall I began
to sway it then they beged for me to come
down they caught it to hold it up and was
begging me to come down after I plagued
them all I wanted to and they had made
all kind of promises if I would come down
when I came down they went for me, was
going to brake me all up, I told Mother
about it she said they ought to be licked
for cutting the tree down for they knew they
could not scare me,

shortly after that, they sent me to school, then I
was in my tenth year, and the school teacher told
mother that I was the sweetest scholar she had, but
I was very mischievous, but I was sly so she could not
punish me, Mother told her not to spare me she told
her to make me mind, and she said she had no
trouble about it, for I would do any thing she
told me too, she said she thought if she told me
to climb up on the ridge pole I would do it
mother told her I certainly would for that is just
what would suit me. Mother said one time I was
on the roof of the barn with Father, that he was
shingling and he was putting on the weather boards
and he put the hammer on the ridge pole and it
slid off he told me to grab it and I started for it
he had just taken the staging all of that side
of the roof and I started for the hammer. Mother
was looking out of the window, she saw me going
and she ran out said she expected to have to
sweep me up with the broom and dust pan, but
I grabed the hammer before it struck the ground
and when I struck she said I stuck the hammer
up, and started around on the other side,

d met Father about half way down, and landed
him in the hammer, went up on the roof again all right
mother told him to send me down he said I was
all right and we put on the saddleboards, and
leaved the roof of, I was in my bare feet and I
took a broom and swept the roof all off after we
took the staging down, when I went in to supper
mother told me if ever I done any thing like that
again she would skin me, I told her it would
kill me, said she did not mean to take my hide
of, While I was going to school we got laughing
one day at a little instance I wont mention, and
the teacher had to dismiss the school and I had
laughed so much I got highstericky and could not
stop she took me in her arms and carried me home
it was but a short distance and put me to bed
sent for Mother when she came I had gone to sleep
and Mother stayed untill I awoke up when I
woke up I was laughing again Mother told me if
I did not stop she would whip me, so I stopped
and next morning when I went to school we
all began laughing again and the teacher gave
me a sound switching and that made me mad I stopped laughing

when the teacher dissmised the school at noon she had her arms around me and I had mine around her neck, we was hugging each other I did not lay up any thing against her for I thought as much of her as she did of me, the next winter I did not have a chance to go to school that was in Oldtown Maine that my folks was living at that time, and the next summer I was in my eleventh year and my Father moored down on the coast to seaport and went a coasting and I done everything I could, I lived with a man most of the time by the name of Megkivery and he had a daughter about my age we was great friends if one was sent after any thing the other would be sure to go also, they where very nice folks, if they got a present for one they would get it for us both, and when I was 13 years old I got put out with Father and ran away went to Belfast about 6 miles from whare Father lived and they thought I had gone to my sisters whare I used to go, when I had any trouble with the folks at home, and they did not look for me, for about a day and a half and my sister she came to Mothers and they asked her where I was, she said she had not seen me, and she almost went crazy to know where I was, then they began to search for me, and all that they could find out that they saw me going aboard a schooner with a Captian but they did not know what the schooner name or Captians name was and I went that trip and the Capt, belonged in Elnsworth about 60 miles from where Father lived, when we anchored in Elnsworth the Capt, told me I could stay aboard the vessel and all the rest went ashore I did not sleep any that night, I fastened up the Cabin door and turned in and the rats began to run and I thought there was 40 horses on deck, and I made up my mind that the wheel of time had stopped and it would never come daylight, but at last daylight came, and I opened up the Cabin and went on deck and in about an hour after the sun arose the Capt, he Came aboard and wanted to know how I got along I told him pretty well, well he said you had better go ashore and get breakfast at the house and I asked him if I had earned anything

I should like to have it for I should like to go home, he said Oh no he wanted me to stay with him but I was aful homesick when we whent into the house the Capt.s wife was a large noble looking woman and she took me right up in her arms notwithstanding I was 13 years old, and the Captin says he wants to go home but she said Oh no you re going to live with us, so she whent to the villiage bought colth to make me some clothes and there was a couple of ladies came to help her and the next day I was togged out with a whole new suit with a boild shirt on, that was something I never had before, we stayed there about 3 weeks had some work done on the vessel and loaded there with lumber for Bristol R. I. and I was fitted all out with bedclothes and everything they could get for me and she made me promise not to leave so I whent with them in that vessel about 2 years during that time I had been 8 times to the West Indies, and the Captain had a new square rigged brig built for him, and we loaded with shooks for Matanstans W. I. and his wife whent with us, and she had

rught books, but I had studied some before
and the Capt had helped me, but when his
wife came aboard with the little libery she sot
me right studding and she helped me, when we
got back to Boston there was Capt Gilkely
came aboard and when he saw me he knew me
and he says to Capt Chase thd was my Capt
name, he says taint thd Charles Hanning, he
says yes thd is his name but we call him Tim
Capt Gilkely said thd was a nickname I went
by, when Capt Gilkely went home to Sirsport said thd
he had found Charles and he told Father who
I was with Father wrote him a sharp letter to
send me home, the Capt told me I told him
to write he would ~~have~~ have to come after me
for I would never go home alone, I felt aful
bad and I told him if I have to leave you I
will never stay at home, Mrs Chase was crying
so the Capt and his wife they both wrote a long
letter to Father stating how well I was getting
along and if he would let me stay with him
thd he would give him one hundred dollars a
year for my wages, and would learn me

comercial business, and Father told him
td I could stay so he sent him one hundred
dollars, after td the Capt; wife and I corrospend
with Mother and she knew where I was we was
loading at td time for Harva France
and we made the trip and came back then we
loaded in New York with supplies for the Government
to go to Verecruise Mexico td was the time of
the Mexican war, and we was laying in the
bay when the city was taken, the crews of
American vessels was drafted out, to stand guard
on the stores td had been landed, by the way the
Capt; took me Mate td trip, then I was in my
17 year and when we whent ashore the Capt; felt
bad his wife was not with us td trip, when we got
in the boat to go ashore the Capt; took me by the arm
and shook me and told me to take care of myself, I
asked him how I could when they would point a
gun at a fellow and shoot it off. and the Officer
he laughed and the men there was two vessels crews
in the boat, the others seemed to be scared to deth
so when they got ashore they dressed us up in line,
and called the roll, and there was 3 chief Officers

in the croud and they told the chief Officers to step
three paces to the front and I stepped out the others
did not, the Officer wanted to know if there was any
other chief Officer I told him there was the chief Officer
the barque E. Wilson and the barque Solutte, he ordered
them to come out and they came very scared, and the
Sargeant Mager came down with an order for the
chief Mates to return back aboard their vessels,
So they could not take the mates out, the Sargent
Mager asked me whare I was from I told him I
was from Elsworth Maine, whare the vessell
sailed from he asked me if I was a son of Capt
John Hanning, I told him I was if my Mother
was an honest woman and I thought she was; he
said I know your Father, he said I lived in
Bellfast, so he took me up to the none commissioned
Officers dinner, and bout 4 Oclock in the afternoon
the chief Officers was sent back aboard their
vessels, and the rest of the men stayed 14 days
when they came of to pay the men, they paid
me the same as the rest; When we left Veacruise
we went to Havannah Cuba, and loaded for
New York, there Charterd for a trading cruise

round the Cape to California, we went to
Alkpucko Mexico, Massisland and Santiagogo
California, we lifte Santiagogo about the middle
of May with salted hides for ballast in 1848
and gold was dicovered in August of thd year,
and we loaded there with cotton for Harva France
and we never knew any thing about the gold being
discovered untill we got to France. We returned
from France with a cargo to New York, then the Capt. go a
charter to go up the Mediterean then we went to
Constantipial Turkey from there we went to old
Alejanderia in Egyept in ballast, there we loaded
with goats hides matting linceed and general cargo,
for New York, we went from New York to
Reiegono Brijils with a general cargo and go
returned from there to New York, with coffe
and general cargo, and the Capt wanted to go
home he wanted me to go in the brig Master as
and the rest of the owners thought thd I was too
young being in my 20 year at thd time, and
they wanted to put an older man in the Capt,
told them if they did they could buy him out
for I was going Master if he owned in her,

So the agent made consultations getting an old Capt, to go mate, and when we got out side I would tell him what I wanted done, he began to turn up his nose, thought that I did not have any thing to say, the third day out in the afternoon I told him what I wanted, he wanted to know who was running the Brig I told him I did not want any of his impidence and it resulted in me sending him to his room, he stayed there about three days and he came to me wanted to go on duty and I told him if he would behave hemself and do as I told him he could go on duty for did not any more truble with him and would not have it, I was bound to Galvastaes & Yexcea's and he done very well the remainder of the voyage untill we got almost there, I over took a Brig in the afternoon which was bound for the same place and he spoke me wanted to know if I was going in that night, the weather looked bad and the wind was to the eastesed; but before I had time to say any thing he spoke up and said No I am not going in, I told him to shut up his head, I told the Capt I was

going in I had found out that he had been
trying to poisen the men against me, also the
second mate, had been calling me the baby Capt,
I told the Mate to go to his room and if he came
out before we got in I would break him all up
and throw him overboard and I went in I got
the lights to bear just right I ran up the river
let go my Starboard anchor let her swing
around let go my port anchor, there was no
wharves there at that time but they had spiles
drove down, and I ran my hossers out on the
port side after I had made fast to the spiel
I brought it in on the Starboard side through
the chocks and made fast and I laid all
right, the next day in the forenoon it stormed
so bad I did not go ashore when the storm
abated there was 7 vessels wrecked on the
outer and inner bar, there was a total loss
when the weather cleared up, I began to
discharge but by the way the Mate says
to me I dont suppose you want me any
longer I told him I did not if he stayed
aboard the vessel he would have a tin cover over his mouth

nd he went ashore worked his passage up to New Orleans
befor the mast, He wrote an aful letter to the agent
stating thd they would never see their vessel again, for
the Capt. was nothing but a baby and did not know as
much as a nursing child, and they was thinking of
sending a Capt down there to get her, but I got away
before they could get one there, but they had one all
ready and when I got in to New York, I wrote to the agent
I had got in, he thought he would come and see me
before they sent the Capt, I asked the agent if he had
got a letter from the mate, he said he had I told
him thd he tried as hard as he could to have
me loose the vessel, by the way thd brig that spoke
me the night before I went in she got all blowed to
peices, when I came out she had just got in between
the two bars and was anchored, and he said he
was blown all to peices had hardly enough sail to
get in with, I saw her in afterwards, and he told me
he thought his last day had come, he was about
four weeks getting back, I showed the agent the letter
thd the shipper gave me, and the man thd I took
for mate told him how I had manged and when
I got discharged the parties wanted me to go back

to Galvestone Texas I asked the agent if he wanted
me to charter the vessel again for Capt Durham
and he said I better charter for myself, that he did
not think they wanted to make a change, so I charted
her and I went down east got the mate I wanted
before and went back, and I had a fine time every
thing went smoothly when I got back to New York
and discharged I loaded for Mantanzee Cuba
and I through a cargo of Molasses back to Boston
and the owners sold the brig and built me a barque
I worked on her she was most done when I got home
and I loaded her for New Orleans with brick & hay
from New Orleans I loaded with staves hogsheads
for Mantanees Cuba again, I took a cargo of sugar
house Molasses up to New Orleans, there I load with
sugar and New Orleans Molasses for New York,
and the owners sold the barque and I went home
and they built another vessel for me that was in the
fanl, I took a square rigged brig went out to
Havannah for a load of molasses for Portland
then the Capt that I went for he took the brig and
I went home, and worked on the barque they was
building for me, About a month before she was

ready I got married, which was a very unfortunate
match, after I was married my wife was bound to go
with me and I told her my vessel was not fitted for a
woman, but she said she did not care she was going
so I told her all right, when I started to go about 2
miles to where my vessel laid I told her I would send
the coach after her to be all ready, and I went to the
stable and ordered the coach when it got to the house
I was about 4 miles down the bay with a stiff breeze
blowing from the North west, but I expected to meet her
in New Orleans but instead I got a letter I did not
think I would hardly dare to return I was gone about
five months, then I returned to New York with a cargo
there was parties wanted to buy the vessel I owned
about four thousand dollars in her and the owners
have me power of Attorney to sell her, and I sold her,
when I got home my wife's brother met me at the
steamboat wharf with a carriage and I told him I
hardly dare go he said he guessed it would be all
right they would be glad enough to see me, so I
saw the agent and settled up with him and we
had a laugh about my going away the way I did
for I told him before I went what I was going to do

my wifes brother came back with his carrige and got
me it was about 2 miles over to her Fathers and they was
all glad enough to see me, I worked on another vessel
intill she was done she was called Globe, and when
I got ready to go away, my wife was not in a condition to go
so I had no more trouble on that account, and was gone
about 7 months I whent to Vercruise Mexico and from there
I whent down the coast and took a load of dry wood
lingivety and black ebeny and other native wood
for Harva France and the consinesse wanted me to
take a portion of the cargo under the main hacth
so to make a port entery of it, I told them that I did
not really understand how to do it they said that
was very easy, but however I whent up to
Vercruise about 25 miles that run to Vercruise
and I saw the American counsel and he told he
would fix it, and he did he told me what to do
by the way he was a frenchman but an naturlije
American, I got my papers all fixed I saild when
I got there and delivered my papers to the custom
house, the men that I was consinged to they wanted
the cargo at once, and I told them there was a
little over thirteen hundred dollars freight on it to pay

they said they would pay the freight after it was
delivered I told them they would pay it before it was
delivered, they said I would have to deliver it before I
could get my other cargo I said decidedly I shall but
I will deliver it to a warehouse, they said that would
do I told them I would put it in a government warehouse
and bond it they said that would not do I said I
guessed it would, I told them if they wanted to pay
the freight before 10 Oclock they could do so, and if not
I should order the government teams down at 1 Oclock,
and they did not pay before 10 Oclock I went to the
custom house and ordered the teams to be there at 1 Oclock
ordered the custom house officer to break the seal and
he did and my men took the hatches off and began to
take out the cargo, and they came down with the freight
money and I told them they would have to pay the
government teams I had engaged and they said they
would not do that so I told the stevedores to load
the teams up and they paid the teams and I discharged the
cargo, the ship chandler who was an American and
he told me there was a Capt Gilleky from Portland main
that they had got about $1400.00 the same way, so I discharged
the balance of my cargo with out any trouble,

loaded there with a general cargo for New York, and
things whent along very smoothly, After I got discharged in N.Y.
I loaded for Shaganess the isthmus of Kinnamass
and from there I whent Cardinis Cuba and loaded with
Molasses for Boston, and I was not well we sold the vessel
I whent home, and had a sever spell of sickness that was
in 1855 and during that year I had met with some very
heavy losses in navagition, by trying to help others
and I started in to build mr fidest brig. and my
domestic affairs became so unbarbable that I settled
up and sold out everything that I had, and left five
hundred dollars with my agent for my children a
Mr Prescott Ajeltine and whent to California, and
I worked at first Sacamurto on the Combination
steamers and they was building a railroad from
Sacarmotta to foltsome mossmar island
and the masterworkman, wanted me to go to work
on the road I left the steamers and whent to work on
the railroad when they got read to put the first
sleeper down I grabbed it up and threw it in its place
and the boss said you can say you are the first man
that ever laid a sleeper in California for a railroad

worked for the railroad untill my health gave out on account
of the water then I went into the mountains and was all right
I went to prospecting and spent all the money I had and
there was a man wanted me to build a barn for him and I
had two pardeners Morse and Williams I earned
provisions they kept on prospecting and one of them
came to me while I was building the barn, and wanted
me to go down on a place called verancycrick there was
deep ravine and we went to work just before we
rocked off we got on a bedrock and took out a panfull of
dirt and we took about $40.00 in gold out of the panfull
d we went and staked of our claim for three which
was nine hundred feet, we was allowed one hundred
yards for each man, then we notified the rest of the
miners that we had struck gold there, and they all
went and took up the balance of the stream, and
built a dam to save our water and went down to the lower
end of our claim and commenced digging first day we got
down on the bed rock and we took out about fifty dollars
and we was offered 3 thousand dollars for our claim
that was one thousand apeice, and we went to work and we
worked up about a hundred foot and never got the
color, we felt pretty blue, I went to the store

had about 15 dollars and I paid that out and got about 27 dollars in debt, and the next day I see something in the sluice box after the dirt had washed away. I reached in got a hold of it and it was a nuget of gold about 90 dollars and we cleaned up we took out about one hundred and forty dollars in all, I paid the storekeeper, and we went back to work and we worked up about another hundred foot and never got the color, and I went down the mountains about 14 miles to see if I could get a job of work I could not find any thing. so a 50 lbs sack of flour and started back I got pretty tired going up the mountain, I kep jogging along, untill I thought I got about opposite to whare the boys was to work and it must have been along the middle of the night and I slipped down going down the mountain and the sack of flour came under my head I went to sleep when I woke up I was almost frozen and it was sometime before I could tell whare I was I straightened up got the flour on my shoulder and staggered of down the mountain, and I got down to the claim just as the boys woke up and we began to get short of food and money after we had worked about half of our claim out and I told the boys that I would hunt up work, So I whent down to a place called Bridlersbar on the North fork of the feather river, where they was building an suspecion bridge I asked the man if he wanted any help, whos name was Williams, he was from Nova Scotia, he said no answered me pretty short, so I whent down about 7 miles below there to a place called Oresville and I could not get any thing to do there I only had five dollars with me, I paid one dollar for my dinner and $.2.5-0 for my supper breakfast and lodgeig so that that left me with only $.1.5-0 when I got back to Bridless bar I whent into the shed hotel I was considering the matter over what to do, to pay $.1.5-0 for my supper and lodgeing (and I had not had any dinner that day) or go to bed with out my supper and pay for my lodgeing and breakfast for I had 14 miles to walk before I could get back to the claim, while I was thinking the matter over Williams the man that was building the bridge came in and said, that he would have to send to Sacammento or San serisfco to get 2 funces of four stranded rigging he said that sailor said 3 stranded rope could not be spliced, and I looked up and said I should

like to see a three stranded roap that I could
not splice, he asked me if I knew how to splice
roap and I told him I had pulled enough to
know how, he says I dont know any thing about
your pulling, but I will give you $. 10. oo if you will
splice it so it will go through the block, we went
down to the bridge what they was building & cut a
narey miller bush almost as hard as iron I whittled
it out for a marlenspike went to work, the fellow had
cut off about half a bushel of the roap and unonlaid
and destroyed it and I took it and put it together
and spliced it in less time than what I have been
writing about it, and I showed it to him and explained
it to him and told him it was stronger there than
any whare else I put it down on a peice of board,
and rolled it with my foot and he looked at it there
was 4 or 5 men a mining clost by and he called them
and asked them if they could tell whare it was put
together they said they could not if they had not
known, and he gave me the ten dollar gold peice
and said he would give me $. 7. oo per day and board
me to take charge of the fauls and derricks to get
the stringers across,

he said he had the prettys wife and two the
prettiest children itd was in California and I think
he told the truth he said he would board me at his
house I told him I did not think I was in a condition
to go to a private house I had been sleeping out theng
had got on my clothes, and he said itd was nothing
he did not belive there was man woman or child in
California but what was lousey, and I worked for him
intill he paid me a little over 7 hundred dollars then
he got me a chance for a hundred and twenty five
dollars per month, getting out fluming timber in
the mountains, he had a man who had charge of his
work he was a very disergable man, and the men did
not like him, I told him I wanted three men the
first day he said I could have more if I wanted
them I told him them would do, and I set them to
work was around with them and this boss came
up and told them to go on another Job I told them
to stay right where they was, and he brusseled up to
me and said if he wanted me to do any thing I
would have to go, says I not much I walked up to
him he began to back, back and he backed up
against a small log and went over, heels over

head, and picked himself up and started off,
and all the men began to lauh and holler he went
and found Williams told him that I was going to
fight him he wanted to know what it was about
said he wanted the men I had, he said did he let
you have them, he said no and that is what I was
going to fight him for, well the boss said if
he was going to take charge (meaneing me) he could
get another man and he told him I have got him
all ready so he paid him off and let him go
and I finished up the bridge, And the men they
thought everything of me and Williams was glad
he made the change but Steel had one man
that was a great friend and he set out to make some
trouble for me and I told him to leave and go with
him if he wanted to, he said he would not for me
he caught up an ape and was going to strick me
with it but one of the men grabbed it out of his
hands at the same time nocked him down and
they had to help him up, and he went of, and
everything went along smootlly after that, untill
the bridge was finished.

then hired with a man by the name of Heartt and
bent up on the north fork and took charge of a crew of
men, to get out fluming timber for to flume the river
sixteen hundred feet and the gang that was getting it out
before I took charge of it, had run three bosses off, and
when they told me that they wanted me to take charge
of the crew they might just as well kill me, as to send
me among them boarder ruffins by the way I had
built a barn for Mr Heartt and he came to me one day
and told me he wanted me to go up in the Mountains
to take charge of that crew that was up there so I bid
them good by and told them to bury me decleant when
they killed me, they said they would, so when I got up
there the men was all out to work or pretending to be at
work and I thought I would go to work and set up a
grindstone it was laying up against the side of the
Cabin when I thought it was near twelve oclock I got
dinner and the men came in a swearing wanted to know
if I had come up there to boss them, I told them I guess
they did not want any boss they could get along without
one, I did not say much of any thing to them the next
morning I got up and got breakfast there was 12
men and I made 13, they wanted to know if I was not

getting up early I told them I was tired of laying so I waited untill they all got up there was one man by the name of William Horton he was a large Buckteering and an offul good fellow so he started out the first one and I went with him, and about an hour and a half they all got out there to work, and worked untill about leven oclock and I made a motion that there was enough to have a cook out of the croud one fellow a Prusrian said he would cook, if I said so says he I suppose you are boss I said if you think I am you may have the Job of cooking and the rest seemed to be well pleased and the next morning I woke him up to get breakfast, so that I started out a little before sunrise and this Horton he followed me and all the rest came right after us, and that was all the trouble I had with them they where all nice fellows and they called me the yankee boss, I dont think there was a man out of the whole twelve but would have fought for me for the least thing and we got our flumeing timber all out and built our road down to the river and then, the boss on the river whos name was Bears and he told me to take my men and go down on the river and grading the claim was

sixteen hundred feet long, and he put about fifty men
in my gang, I had the upper seyction, and I graded
up to the upper end of the claim there I had a large
bluff, to blast off, and I proposed to the cheif boss
to go right back as far into the bluff as we wanted
to and put some deep holes and blast it off in the
deep water that was under the bluff, and he told one
to go right in on the face of it and blast out and
gave me a pretty short answer, I told him maby
you dont want me any longer and he said he did
not unless I did as he told me too well I said get
my money for me just as quick as you can he had
about 12 miles to go down to Bridlesbar to the office
so I took my gang went back where I wanted to I
put down 3 deep holes with churn drills, and one
was 19 ft deep the other was 21 ft the other was 23 ft,
and I got them down the afternoon and charged them
and touched them off that night, and I opened it the
hole length of the bluff, about 15 inches, and the
water came into the bottom, the next morning I
set all the men to work cutting boughs to throw
into the bottom of the seam and then I threw clay
and sand in untill it was dry,

ten I put 75 lbs of powder in flour sacks and put my fuse in and let it down into the hole which was about 8 ft I put 3 fuses all of a length, and then packed it with sand and clay itd I had at hand, I packed it down hard and just as I got ready to touch them off I saw Mr Heartt and Mr Burst comeing down the Mountain, we was on the oppiste sid of the river from the boarding house and we had a roap suppescion bridge across the river, and they was comeing across, and I beckond to them to keep back, and everybody was runing for shelter, I had three men with a live coal to touch the fuse off, and when it went off, it laid the whole bluff right over in the water in to build the floom on, and they came across after it flowed it off, and Burse and Heartt came up Burse says well you Yankee you did do did, ent you, I did not say any thing to him Mr Heartt came up and shook hands with me I said I suppose you are ready to settle with me, Oh no he said I said did you not come up to discharge me Oh no no, I said I thought Burse went down after you to come up and discharge me, no he said that was not the intention I looked him in the face and told him to tell me the truth, he asked me if I would stay if he would, I told I would, and he said he did come with that intention, but he did not want me to go Bruse wanted to shake hands and make up, and let it all pass, so I played there was a bluff down about two thirds of the way whare the other bosses gang was it was no way to blow it off down in the stream, so we went down to look at it that; they did not hardly speak to the other boss, they was blasting right in on the face of it would not blast out more than a bushelbasket full at a time, they wanted to know what I would do there, and I told them I would go right in back as far as they wanted to go, put in three holes just the same as I did up to the head and break away so as to loosen it up and then we could blast in from the face, and break it up in large peices they told me to come down and do it, and the gang at that time had all gone to dinner, and the boss, of the gang got mad, did not go to work that afternoon when we went to supper, he had been drinking and he was a big stout young man by the way he belonged to Quincey Mass, his name was McGregory and he was going to clean the whole boarding home out and he had cleaned them all but me I was laying in my bunk and he went for me, I jumped out of my bunk quick and knocked his feet out from under him

nd he came down on his face I lit on his back and
caught his hands and fetched them up, and I made him
beg before I let him up, just dusk in the evening and he started
off diggin in on camp budy, he was gone two and a half
days & we began to think he had commited susicide
they was talking about linching me because I was the
means of him commiting Susicide, and the third day
just before noon he came back on the river where
I was to work and said he had made a fool of
himself, I told him maby the Almighty done it first
nd he wanted me to go and see the main boss, Mr Bur
see if he would take him back and he said it would
be all right to tell him to go to work again and things
went along smoothly untill we got the flume built,
nd I left and went up in the mountains further
to a place called longbar on the north fork of the
feather river, and put in water wheel and a pump
we tried to get down on the bed rock, and made a
failure, there was five of us in company and the
other three we left, two of us worked the surface of
the river and made about twenty three hundred
dollars apeice in about seven weeks, and it got to be
in the faul about the first of November.

nd there was a man carreing on butchering and wanted
me to go in with him he offerd me one half of the business
if I would go in partnerships with them, and I accepted the
offer and it had got so late that they had drove their cattle
all down in the Sacrmanto valley and I had to go down
there and got cattle to carry us through the winter, I
bought nine stears they would weigh about seven
hundred a peice dressed, and it looked in the vally
very much like rain, when I started for the
mountains which I had about 45 miles to go I
drove 21 miles the first day then I drove 14 miles
the next day that was 34 miles of the 45 I had eleven
miles further to go and it was snowing in the mountain
when I started the further I got up the deeper the
snow grew, when I got where I turned of the
emergrant road to go over the summit of the
mountain I "woof" sent the man back with the two ponies
we had and I drove the cattle as far as they would
go and I made up my mind that I had to leave
them I had about two miles further to get over the
summit and I knew when I got over the summit
that I could strike down on the river get out of the
snow, the snow on the summit was about 3 ft dp

when I started to leave the cattle they trailed right
along after me and I got down to whare the snow was
about 8 inches deep I came to whare there was a big fur
tree there was bare ground under it when the cattle
saw that they laid down on the bare ground, and I
had a box of matches and a parifine candel and
fortunately there was an old windfall close by
I broke some limbs off and made a fire, I kut the
candel in two and lit it and placed it in the limbs
and started a fire for I was wet all through when I got
a little warm, the cattle laid down so close together
I would lay down between them one side would get
so cold I would get up and lay down on the other side
the cattle would not move it was about 2 Oclock in
the morning when I got under the tree and at daylight
it cleared off I could see whare the sunrose and struck
my course on the edge of the snow for the trail, which
I had got off when I struck the trail I was about 4
miles from the bar, I drove the cattle along until
they could hear me on the bar, soon as they heard me
too bymen came and met I tought I was all right
untill I saw them then I collaseped and they
helped me down on the bar that was the last of drove

and I never whent out again untill April I sent for
a Dr about 24 miles, and he charged me $.90.00 for
the first visit befor I got out I paid twentyone
hundred dollars for Drs bills, and I sent to Sacrementy
to a Dr I was aquainted with and stated my case and he sent
me medicine and directions and I began to get better right
way, my partener was an very nice man, about 55
years old whos name was M' Shane a scotchman
he would wait on me like a Mother, but he drank offuly
and let the business all go to the hired man, and when
I got out our stock was all gone and we had about
fourthousand dollars standing out, and no money to
repelinsh, and the fellow that worked for us left
to go home to St Louise mouseria, when he got aboard
the steamer at Santafrices he sent his compliments
to us and said he had a thousand dollars of our money
and we would never get, I told them I hoped he would
die with the asiatic colhar befor he got home and
he died with the yellow fever in New Orleans, I settled
up with my partner and turned over everything but
one horse and saddle and started about 25 miles
further up the river, to a place called Indian valley
with 48 dollars and the horse, and I put up to a

publice house, and met an old friend that I had been on the jury with, in a murder case he wanted to know what I was going to do, I told him I did not know I had not much money and only a horse, I supposed I should have to sell the horse he said you stay here untill I come back and he told the landlord to charge my bills to him and rode of with my horse and the next forenoon he came back with about seven hundred dollars he had got off the miners about seven miles blow there, and told me to start buthering and if I wanted any more money he would collect it for me, that afternoon I went over across the neck of the valley where a man had a ranch I had got two men to put up a gallos where I could dress cattle while I was gone and I bought five stears I paid eleven cents a pound on foot and we judged them at a certian weight as I had been in the business before I could judge the weight of the cattle great deal better than the man that I bought them of could so I got the better of him to about a hundred and seventy five pounds on every stear, that night when I got back I killed and dressed one of them I had no trouble in selling all out that night and the next day, and I bought an old waggon and fitted it up I got a double harness from an emergrant that had crossed the plains and he wanted money so he let me have it very cheap and I fitted up a butcher waggon and started peddling beef around the valley and I would go one way about twelve miles then I would go the other way about the same distance the other way, I would go about every third day each way by going one way one day and going the other way the next day, this was about the last of May I started buiseness in about seven weeks I had money enough to pay my seven hundred dollars and I had seven head of cattle all paid for and continued untill about Xmas, and the mineing buisiness all closed up in the mountains and the miners all went down to the foot hills and I closed up my buisiness and crossed a range of mountains over to medow valley where the county seat was, and started buisiness there, and there was one firm that had spent about fifteen thousand dollars they was owing me six hundred dollars, when they got their tunnel in to where they wanted to go they had sunk a shaft previous to that whare ninty odd ft deep and struck water then they had to go in to the side of the Mountain to start a tunnel, and when they got in to whare the shaft was they was too low and they had to drill up they got in about six inchs and struck water they tried another place got in about the same distance and struck water, then they drilled in as far as they dare to and got in a light charge and touched it off, but they was careful and got out of the tunnel before it went off and when the water started it was seven miles from Quincey California county seat, and we heard the water rushing all the distance we did not know what it was, untill the evening a man came over from rush creek and told us what it was, those parties had a reservoria and a ditch that was woth about seven thousand dollars and they rigged a highdraulick hose and started to wash down, and they washed down two and a half days, and they got clear out to the mouth of the tunnel and never saw the color of gold, and one of them John Gowdigle he came over to Quincey to get some supplies a man by the name of Wilber kept a grocery store they was owing him about a thousand dollars and me

about six hundred and Wilber he would not let them
have any more supplies and Yowliger was about discouraged
I asked him what he wanted to make out a list of what
he wanted he did I had a back half layin on the
butcher block I put a knife on it about a half
peice and he said he did not know as he could ever
pay me I told him it did not make any odds I
would not be as big a looser as they had been, I
bought beans and bacon fifty tbs of flour and
coffee and sugar every thing he wanted and he
started back with the boy and the pack mule
and he had not been gone more than a half hour
before the expressman came in a hollering we all
ran out to see what the matter was finaly we got
him cooled down he got out Yowliger and
Thompson and Leo, the richest men there was in
California, that they had cleaned up a hundred
thousand dollars that morning, everybody got
on their horses and mules and started over where
they was, when we got over the gold was in a pan
and the pan was all most full when they weighed
it there was a little over twenty three thousand
dollars, when they got down to the mouth of the

claim where the revet was in the sluice boxes they
began to see the gold, that was after Travelighn had
left to come over to Quincy, he did not know any thing
about it untill he met the expressman, that was
about the middle of June 1858 and the 4 of July
they had cleaned up about one hundred and seventy
thousand dollars they had been offered a million
dollars for it, but I noticed I was the first one that got
my money I had about four hundred dollars in bills I
told them I would leave it with them for collecting
and the firm talked the matter over took the bills
paid me the money, and my health got poor and
I settled up and started for Sanscrifeo, got down to
Marysville and the state fair was going to be there the
next week and I could not get a room any where and there
was a man by the name of Jim McnaB one of the worst
desperadoes there was in California, when I went to
California three years before that, I was with a
Dr Morron from New Hampshire that lived in
Sacamento and he wanted to exploi the table
mountains in Costarica her Cnctral America
and he left his family at Vergen bay nigerogulake
and we went into the mountains on the table Mountai

we was gone about two weeks and when we got back
to Venarden where we took the steamer to go to
bergenbay they told us the passengers was on the
pacific side that was left to go up the coast
when we crossed the isthmus of nigerogen we met
the passengers that we left New York with, and Mr
Murrown joined his family his wife and two child
and brother and sister and we stayed there about 3
days before we got away, Walker was down there a
fella bustlering and this McnRab was with him and
the mate of the steamer that we went up in had
left the steamer and gone home to N.Y. Mr Murrel
was one of the pricipal owners in the company so
he got me the second mates bilt as the second
mate had taken the mates place, and this
McnRab got wounded in the leg had to go back to
Sancrifeeo and he had no accomaditin aboard
the ship I had two bunks in my room I took
him in with me and kept him the whole passage
of 14 days and the asahicate colhen broke out on
the ship the second day out from Sanwasnfollsiid
and we lost three hundred and fifty four in
about twelve days, and McnRab thought there

was no one like me, When I got into Sanсисfico I
found out who he was and everybody told me to be
carlful of him and get clear of him as quick as I
could one fellow told me I was just as safe with
him as I would be with my mother, so he took me
around and showed me the town would not let me
spend a cent of money I went in about three
weeks from Sancaserifco down to Pannanfar
the second mate of a steamer when I came back
I went up in the mountains which I have
spoken about before, I did not see any thing more
of Mᶜnay until I came down I found him
at Marsville where he got his living by
gambling the rooms was all taken up he made
me go in his room with him he told me if I had
any money to put it into the safe I told him I
wanted it me to pay my bills, he said your
bills will get paid you do as I tell you and
the clerk told me it would be all right so I
put what I had in the safe afterwards the clerk
told me to be careful not to get in any trouble
with any body for he said Jim would shoot
them in a minute if any one insulted me

after I had located my room with my friend Marab
I went around to see some of my aquintances and
friends and the Mayor and his two partners
the Mayors name Height and his partners names
was Deaher and Smith, they was building a bridge
across the Nabea river and I went into their store
and Smith wanted to know if I wanted a job on the bridg
I asked him what he paid he said seven dollars a day
I told him I would go to work, so I reported that
afternoon when I got on the job, I found that Steel
was boss he did not know me at first, and he gave
me a gang of men on a portion of the bridge the
next frenoon he discovered that I was the man
that had superseeded him on the other bridge
and he took me off and put me in the gang carring
heavey plank across a diffluelt place, I told him
I would not do it he said I could leave I told him
he could go where they did not rake up fire over
night I had worked three quarters of a day and I
went to the office and got my money just as I
was going out of the door I met Judge Eva
and all three of the partners rushed to speak to
him and the Judge gave me an introduction to

the same men I had been working for, and the Judge took me by the shoulder and shook me and said to the Mayor and his partners, this is one of natures honest men, he has left the Mountains without owing a dollar. Smith says he has been to work for us on the bridge, well says the Judge he is a mechanic every inch of him and a capable man, so Mr Smith said he wanted me to go back on the bridge again and I told him my trouble with Steel at British bar and I would not work under him, says he you go back and I will give you a gang of men you wont have any thing to do with him, so I went back and he took about seventy five men out of Steels gang there was about one hundred and twenty five in all he had, he told Steel that he wanted me to take them and go on the other end of the bridge he said I could take the whole gang if I was going to do that. Smith said ill right Mr Hanning I want you to take charge of the whole gang, says I all right, and Steele left and I went on with the finishing up of the bridge, and the next day, they was looking for the first arrival of the folks to come to the state fair I put on all the men that I could get when it came night—I asked the men if they would work all night and they all readily agreed and the next morning I had one side of the bridge so they could cross and just as I laid the last plank down on that side there was a team on the other end of the bridge and they began to pour in and Smith and Decker came down about 8 Oclock, and they saw the teams coming they came up and caught me by the hand and congratulated me with doing so well said they had made a good change. And about 11 Oclock Judge Eva came down with all three of them and at noon they said they had dinner all ready waiting for us and we went up to the Shade Hotel, there I met my friend McNab again and I told them in a brief interview the circumstances how I came to get acquainted with him, and what he had done, the Mayor and his party knew all about him they told me to invite him to dinner and I gave him an introduction to Judge Eva and he behaved like a gentleman after dinner he excused himself went off. but told me before he went that he did not want to stay with my company they was too respectfully for him

and I laughed and told him all right. I finished
up the bridge the next day the fair commenced
and we nocked off for two days for the fair then I
finished up the bridge, the first day the men
nocked of for the fair I saw Steele coming out of
a drug store with his head all tied up, some of
the boys had got abord of him and beat him up
pretty badly, after I finished up the bridge I went
to Santa Frise said I was not very well at the time
I went to see a Dr Cooper a schoolth Dr and he
examined me and wanted to know if I had a
thousand dollars I told him it did not make
any odds to him so long as I paid my bills,
well he said if I had he could keep me there and get
every dollar of it but he could give me a subscribtion
for five dollars that would do me as much good as
for a thousand but he advised me to take a trip
across the Pacific Ocean, and I went to look for a
vessel to get a passage to China there was but
one vessel going there the Capt wanted a second
mate but would not take a passenger so I made
a bargin with him and went abord the
Barque, for Honghong China

and we sailed I dont remember the date it was some
time in July 1858 and our cargo was dead and alive
chinaman about four hundred there was about half
dead bodies and their ashes, every thing went smoothly
and we could not get a freight in Hong hong so we
went to Perterve a ducth Island in the archepelig
called Jarvar, and loaded for Sanfrisanco we
went down through the Philippine Island from
Hong hong to Perterva, and busniss was very
dull and the Capt. was not making any money
in fact he was loossing, and he was quite bilious
and disergable, and he and I had a little conflab
and I had no more trouble with him untill we got to
sea again but he was very abusive to the mate
the mate was a very nice man, but he had no
backbone and he stord his abuse, but I told
him if ever got abroad me he would get all that
belonged to him, in our passage back to
Sanfanciso we carried way our main
topmast just daylight in the morning, and
we cleared up the wreck and had a spare
topmast on deck, got ready to send it up I asked the
mate if he was not going to send down the main yard

and he did not give me any answer, we got the topmast
started just got it into the cap we could not get it any
further I stood looking on the Capt. told me to help
heave on the capstain, I told him it was no use that
we would have to send down the maine yard, and
I told him flatly that I would not help heave on
the capstian, and he said the ship was in a state
of munity he shoot—he went in and got his revolver
I went to my room and got mine when I came out
he wanted to know what I had that revolver for I
told him that he said the ship was in a state of
munity and the first man that stowed any sings
of it I would work seven holes through him and
the Capt. turned white and trembled like a leafe
and told me to go to my room, says I all right—
and he changed his mind told me to go foward I
told him I would not then he told me to go to
work and send up the topmast I told him with
a D. that any fool ought to know it would not go up
without the maine yard was unshipped and the
truss band sung around, I told him if he would
let me have my way I would do it and he said
go ahead so I took charge hauled the topmast

back and lowered it on deck and unshipped the main
yard swung the truss band around and sent the
topmast up got the head of it through the Cap on
the mainmast and sent the topmast rigging up
and sent the maintopmast home put in the fid
in the heal and shipped the main yard again
reaved of my topmast rigging sent the taglemast
royalmast up and put the rigging on and sat it
up temporaily sent my topslandyards up and
bent the sail and had upper and lower topsails
on about half past nine Oclock, and it was my watch
at 8 Oclock so at half past nine I turned in and
was pretty tired and the Capt. told the Mate not to
call me at twelve he would take the watch, so he
did not and it was seven bells the next morning
when I woke up I asked the mate if he called me
he said no the Capt. ordered him not too, I told
him I did not care any thing about what the Capt.
said when it was my watch on deck I wanted
to be called and the Capt. heard what I said when
they went to breakfast he told the Mate that I
was the second Californian that he had for an
Officer and he considered his life in Jafordaes

all the time he had the first one and he considered
his life in jeapardony ever since he left Patavera says
he He would shot me yestirday in a minute if I had
offered to raise my revolver, and the mate told him
he thought I would, he said when he got into
Sanasacrifico if he ever did alive he would let me
go and we got along smortly all the rest of the voyage
when he got into Sanacrisfico he told me he did not
want me any longer wanted to know if I would stay
and discharge the vessell about the time we got
discharged there was a Boston vessell came in and
I saw by the paper that it was the ship Lucknow
Capt, Gorman and I was aquainted with Capt Gorman
he was a particular friend of mine and I went to see
him he wanted to know if I had a vessell there
I told him no he says I have discharged my mate
and I want you to go with me so I packed up my the
stormbird Capt Robbison and told him I would
settle and he said he thought I was going with him
the next trip, I told him I had a friend that
wanted me to go with him so I shipped as mate
of the Lucknow and the very last of December
we sailed for Mellbourn Australia

onst we had a fine passage of about 47 days, we made
the passage from land to land in 37 days, and we was
ten days after we got in the straits of Lamara before
we got to Mellbourne, and from there we went around
Cape Leouine southern part of Australia up through
the Straits of Gaspar to Angampoint and from there
to Java heads from there to Seankpaunpaw, and
from there through the straits of Malakawa up
Ababaka and from there we had orders to go to
Callacutta India, and we laid there three months,
by the way we got loaded in two months and hauled
out in the stream and there came up a terrific wind
and we collieded with two other vessels and got
cut down our minniamast spung and we hauled
back into moorings and laid a month longer in all
we was three months there before we got away, and we was
a hundred and twenty four days from Calluetta to
Boston, we got in Boston the first week in January or
about the middle with our crew all frost bitten and
nine men where to the Hospitial frozen, and I
went to Belfast, where my children was, and
commenced proceeddings for a divorce from my
first wife and took my children at once

and put them out from their Mother I had been
paying my childrens board for five years through
my agent, and my brother inlaw that became
afterwards through the marrige of my second wife
wanted me to take his barque and go to Mantansas
Cuba which I did. When I got back to N.Y. the
civial war broke out, and the Capt came on to N.Y.
and took his barque and I went home to Belfast
that was in 1860 and I was going to Liverpool England
but my Laywer told me I better not go untill after
the May court so my agent told me he wanted me
to take charge of building a brig for him that he
was building for one of his Captains so I did.
And the same Capt, Russ of the barque Laura Russ,
the same vessell I went to Mantansas Cuba in
wanted me to take his barque again and go to Cardise
Cuba, and I did and when I got back the civial
war brok out and I enlisted in the army in Co. E.
fourth Maine Regmenent, and I was in every fight
but Gettersburge from the first bull run in
1861 up to the second day in the Wildeberness
I was wounded twice at the first battle of
Frederickburge the first time, I had my

right shoulder discolated and taken a prisoner and carried to Libby prison in Recomond Vinigina. thore are the battles I was in. The first Bullrun seige of yorktown, Williamaburge, Chichentomeny, Fair Oakes, Seven pines, Savvage station, White oakeswamp, Charlls city cross roads, Rents courthouse, Malvan hill, White oake bridge, Rappah station, Belals station, Cubarun, Second bull run two days, Chanelorville, chantille, Whiteaford, first Gredersburge, seend Gledersburge, Chansroville, Kellys ford, Brandy station, Woolmountain, Racknoonford, and first and second day in the Willindemess, where I was wounded in the head, and that ended my fighting, that was the 6 day of April 1864. And it was 14 days from the time I was wounded untill I got to Washengton I never recolleted any thing dureing the whole 14 days, When I got to the Hospitial on Merdian hill Washington the Dr gave me some medicine too moove my bowels and the next morning I came to myself. but I could not recollect any thing I could not till what my name was or what regmenient or Co I belonged to untill I was told,

Previous to my going to the war I went on with my divorce case and succeeded in getting my divorce in the spring of 1860. and they sent the wounded from Washington to Philidelphia and it was 21 days after I was wounded before my head was dressed in was in McMullean Hospital and the head Dr came in the hospital for to examine the wounded and the Dr told him about me, I was on the dangerous list, so he examined the wound had previously healed over but it was all broke out that morning and the Dr examined it and found that the ball had went through the shull, well up over the right eye and went around on the inside of the shull just above the ear **Lodged** in the thick part of my shull in the back of my head, and they probed and finily trappaned it and made a nice job. then they thought I would not live I fainted away twice from the very reason I would not take ether, the second time I fainted when I came out I came to consheness and could hear what the Dr said and he said if I fainted the third time that I would go I would not come out of it, and I heard what they said and I said I am not going to, and they put me on a stretcher took me out in the ward and put me on my cot, and I could not eat any thing they gave me light liquid food sucked in a glass tube, the third day after my head was dressed they brought me some beef tea and I tasted of it there was about a gill and I drank it all and asked if they had any more they said yes I could have all I wanted, they brought me a lot more and I lived on that for about three day taking a pint at a time, then they began to give me solid food and I recruited right up, that was somewhere about the last of May 1864. The old Dr told the ward Dr that he wanted him to bring me down to Philadelphia to the Office, he wanted to see me so I went down with Dr Curtis the ward Dr and the old gentleman had a long talk with me and said I had one chance in a thousand I told him that was the one I took, and he said in all his proffessional experience that he never a man that exhibited self will as I did, he said it was what saved me, and I went back to the Hospital again and the 15 of June my regiment time was out the fourth maine, and I wanted to go home, they sent me to Philadelphia

I supposed I was going home and they sent me back to Washington and from there to the districting camp in Virginia Arlington Heights, and I made inquiries I could not get any satisfaction, they told me to go to a woman, to see her tell her the facts when I see her she had an office in how I suppose and she answered me quite short, said she did not know anything what to do, I turned around itrubly and walked off when I came back the Sergeant had detailed me to go out and build a fence and I told him to go where they did not rake up fire over night, and I when to General Hanleemen head quarters which was in command at the camp, I asked the guard if I could see the general, he saw the general and he told him to admit me, and I told him who I was and the circumstances, he caught hold of my hand and shook hands with me, said he recollected the further maine regement, said he saw by the paper that their time was out they had left the front, and he told his orderly to bring both of the horses up and when the horses came to the headquarters he gave me a note where to go in Washington to get transurtation home, he told me to get on that horse

and told his orderly to go with me over to Washington
about 7 miles, and when I got my transportation I went
down to the depo and the fourth Maine regiment was
there waiting for transportation, and I stayed with
them until the cars started sometime in the night.
The next morning we was in Baltimore and I left
the regiment there and went on the regular train
with my transportation ticket,—the next morning I
went to the depo in New York found my regiment
there but I went in a different train to Boston,
When I went to the Boston Maine depo the next
morning I found my regiment there, but I
took the train and went to Augusta Maine, there
I took the stage coach went across the country
about 42 miles to Belfast, I arrived in Belfast
about 1 Oclock the next morning, I went to my
old boarding house, and I woke up the lady by
ringing the door bell, she came to the door wanted
to know who was there and I told her, she said it
could not be possible for I was reported dead, well I
told her I was the liveist dead man you ever saw
it is me; she had 2 daughters young ladyes and
they got up they said it was uncle Tommie,

for they knew his voice, so they opened the door and
they found no trouble in recogsing me, there was quite
a bustle for a little while the girls Mother told the girls
not to smother me to death, so then they let up on me then
it was sometime before they would let go off me, for I
looked so natural, they rushed out to the neighbours
the nearest ones had woke up and heard what was
going on and they rushed in and the house was allmost
filled to over flowing, so about daylight I laid down to
get a little nap but I did not lay long so many came
in I had to get up and dress, and about 8 Oclock I went
up town most everyone had found out that I had
got home, and some even wanted to know if I was house,
in a box, they said they guessed not, they said they
saw where I had died they said I was a pretty live
dead man that was I think the 3 of July 1864, and after
I had seen the folks I thought I would go and see my
fairhaired girl, which was the one I wanted to see
most of all, and there was a man took me in his
buggy carried me up to her house, which was
about a mile where her Father lived and they
was expecting the fourth Maine regement —
home that day, for two companys of it —

belonged in Belfast my girl was out to one of her
neighbours when she whent in the woman wasa crying
she asked her what she was crying for and she says
have you not heard the news and she said no, so she
showed her the paper, she said before she had time
to read my death the woman screamed and says there
he is out there in the carrige, and it was but a little
ways to my girls house, and they rushed over I met
them and then she did not really realise about my
death, and this woman grabbed me and my girl said
why Mrs Wright what was you crying for, and she said
she had just saw in the paper where I was dead,
my girl says I was glad I did not see it, and after
my friends had seen me I settled down, but
I had not got the bandage of my head, my two
children was living about 6 miles in the country and
they had heard I was dead, they had their cry and
when the boys that belonged to the two companys
and belonged out in the country was going home that
day when they whent by the house where my
children was, they asked them about me being
dead they said they guessed not for they had
seen me about an hour and a half before that

I was about as live a man as they had seen the next
day I went out to see my children, and the 19 of July
1864 we was mustered out in Rockyland Maine and
we offered our servecies to form a battery we telagraped
to the Governer in Agusta Maine he telagraphed back
to form our battery. We elected our officers and men
34 in number and then we elected our officers I got 32
votes for Captian, and about an hour after we got
a despatch that they could not accept us as battery
but would as infentry, and we did not want to go as
infentry so we disbanded after I had recruited up
I went to East Boston and in a few days I got in
the nevey yard to work and I worked there about
a month and went down to Belfast and got married,
and came to Charlstown and boarded through the
winter, and the next summer my old agent that I
had sailed ressels for came after me to go to Liverpool
England and get a ship, that they had turned the Capt
out of. I went in her about a year and a half and she
was sailing under an english register and I did not
like it so the owners sold her to an english house
and I went back in the navey yard to work. I
stayed there about three years

after I came out of the navey yard I went on to
Piladelipia took charge of putting a sugar deck on a
barque for my brother inlaw, when the men came to work
they was going right in to tear her all to pieces, I told
them what to do, they said they wanted to do different I
told them to do just what I said and there was five
of them, I asked them whare their lumber was they
said that there was not any lumber ordered, I
asked them what they was going to work with they
said they came to tear out so as to get ready I
told them I want you to fetch your lumber here first
and I will tell you what to do, and they went back
and reported to the boss, there was nothing for them
to do untill the lumber got there and he came
aboard in a blustering way wanted to know what
I wanted done, I told him I wanted the
lumber I had ordered then says I you can
send your men, he said he supposed the men
had to tear out to get ready for it I said I told
you what I wanted and I want it if you are
going to do the job then you can send your men
on board, he said he had sent the men
I said did you send them to wait here on

expenses untill the lumber come, he said there
was work enough to do untill he could get the lumber
I told him what there was to do and I knew just
what there was to do, and if he could not do it I
would get some one else he said if he knew what
I wanted done he would do it, then I told him to
look at the statement I had made out, he said
it was at the office I said is that the way you do
take a statement and lay it away and then do as
you have a mind to, but you have got to do just as I want
you to for I will take the vessell, and go to Boston so he
went and ordered the lumber, and the men came down two
of them to go to work one worked about a half an hour and
went away in about a half an hour the other one went
and was gone about an hour and a half, when they came
back I asked them what they had been doing and
they said that was not any of my business say well
it is and you get ashore just as quick as you can and
they went ashore, and the boss came down wanted to
know what the trouble was I told him one worked
about a half an hour and the other one about an hour
and went of was gone about an hour and a half to two
hours and I had their time, they would only get

pay for what time they was there, and need not send them two men back to me I told him I wanted men there by 1 Oclock or I would clear for Boston, and they did not get down untill about a quaten of 2 Oclock I sent them back and went up to the agent and cleared for Boston when I got back aboard the vessel the boss was there I told him the men did not get there untill about a quater of 2 Oclock and I would not love them, there was one big fellow he went and brought him back he said he was there at 1 Oclock I told him he did not get there untill a quater of 2 Oclock and he told me I was a d—m,liar, and he felt the end of my arm and went heals over head, when he got up he had his hand on his face, and was making for the warfh, I told the boss I had cleared for Boston and he could take his lumber away and make out his bill for one hour and a half's work, he said he would attach the vessel for full pay, I told him to go ahead, I had engaged the tug to tow me out the next morning to port-Richmond to load with coal for Boston, and he said I will do the work and do it as you want it I will come here myself and see that the men is here on time and he did, and the next morning six men came on time, I told them what I wanted done and they done it and I got the carpenter work all done, and the calkers they came on, and they tried the same thing thd the carpenters did and I discharged them, then the boss came again and wanted to know what the trouble was I told him they was trying the same thing thd the carpenters did, and I discharged them I should only pay them for what time they worked by the hour and half hour, he said at 10 Oclock I will send men here thd will work and he would come with them himself, they came down and what to work and finished up the Job sasictafory, and I told the boss to make out his bill and the bill came he had full time, for all hands I told him now there is my bill we compared them, there was about five days difference. I told him I would not pay it untill he settled my bill, then he said he would libale the vessel, I told him to go ahea and I would get bonds, so he said he would split the difference and call it 2½ days, I told him I would not do it thd he would have to settle at my bill, and he did,

and I paid him, he told me I better be careful
about being around town for the men was laying
for me, I told him if any of them wanted to see
in that line to tell them to bring an undertaker
with them, but I did not meet any trouble, and I
loaded the vessele for Pencolia Florida with coal
and sent for the Captain and he came on and took
her and I came home, I had another brother in law
in the vessele and he got in to Baltimore and sent for
me to come on and take her, and discharge her, get
a load of coal for Portland Maine, and I did go on
and take her. when I got to Portland, the Captian
came and got her there and I came home again,
that was in 1869 and I was living at Charlstown at
the time and I moved from Charlstown to E. B.
and went to keeping boarders on Meridian St-
between Central square and London St- and after
I got the house running, I went and laid the
launching ways for an iron Brig. that was
launched sideways, after I got the ways laid
I went to work on deck, and I met with an accident
I fell 23 ft, and it laid me up for quite a while,
when I got well I went on a finished the Brig

she was built for to carry mollasses in bulk, Capt, Gustin Havener commanded her; after she sailed I went at carpentering, and Mr Snow and Sons of Boston wanted me to take a schooner to go to Rearogenero Brizill, and I refused and they told me if I would take her they would build me any kind of a vessele that I wanted when I got back and I wanted to dreadfully, but my wife would not let me go and I gave it and in 1870 I got burnt out in the big fire of E. B. and whent over to Boston and opned another boarding house, on essex St, and kept thd a year and a half in 1872 I sold out thd house and whent in the grocery buisness but thd prove very unfornate and I lost heavely but sold out of thd business and whent into real estate business and I done well for a year and a half and the panic times came on and I lost heavely in that on second mortggas, and I whent out of that whent to collecting for a firm on Devonshire St, Danfield & Horeskall and Co, I was in their employ about a year, when they failed and one deal while I was with them, they sent me to Phildelphia to collect a bill of about fifteen thousand dollars, when I went into their Office and showed them my credentials, they told me they could not do anything for me and I asked them when they could and they told me that they did not know, and I told them I had come some ways and I wanted some Sacisfaction, they said that they had give me all the sasifaction that they would and to go out, I asked if they thought of putting me out, I told them if they did they had quite a Job, finally I went out and told them they would hear from me soon, I went out on the St, a little way and I saw a sighn Attorney at Law, I went in his Office to consult him I told him what I wanted after he got all out of me that he wanted to he told me he was retained as counsel for those parties and I went in the air and I asked why he did not tell me before, and he says friend dont get epicited maybe you came to the right one and he gave me a note to another firm two young men that was lawyers, and he sealed a note and I went out and did not know what to do I almost thought of commiting suiside, vinally I went in their office handed one of then the note, he looked at it and read it and made the remark

tld was curious then I did not know and he
showed it to his portener and he made the same
remark finialy he asked me what I thought of
doing I told him I had come there to consult
him, well says he I should put a keeper right in
the store, so we talked the matter over and one said
to the other you make out the attachement papers
Capt Hanning and I will go out and see the Sherif
we did and made the arragements at about half
past eleven A. M. we went in the store with two
keepers and in a little while the sheriff he came in
and inquired about different things and what the
price was and the Lawyer and I went into the
Office, I told them I have returned again they
said it was no use, I told them I thought it
was some importance to me if it was not to them
for I had an attachement and the Sheriff right in
the store to close it up and then they came to theirfees
and went in the back office and consulleted each
other came out and wanted to know if I would not
take part of it, I told them no I would have the
whole or none wanted to know if I would take
a cheque on Wall St Bank in New York

and I told yes if was good I asked them what the
Bank was they told me the Lawyer and I went out
and telegraphed to find out if the money was there
and they said it was, I asked them if they would
hold it subject to a cheque untill 11 oclock the next
day, they said they would, and I took the cheque
and the next day I was there with my cheque and
parties to recognise me, and they wanted to know
if I wanted the money or a cheque I told them if
they would give me a chashier cheque on a Boston
Bank I would rather have it, they gave me a cheque
on the Franklin Bank in Boston and I came back
to Boston, I had some business to do in Providence R.I.
for the firm, so when I got back to Boston the store
was closed and I went home to E.B. the next
morning I went over to Devonshire st. to the
store Mr Danfield was reading the morning
paper, he looked up said good morning cast his
eyes down again, says to me you did not have
any luck I said how do you know why says
he they have faild, I said I don't care if they
have and handed him the cheque, and he read
it and screamed rightout as loud as he could holla

he held the cheque up and shook it and the men in the store they ran to the Office and I had a hold of him I told them to take hold of him with me says I the man has gone mad in a short time he cooled down and I told him what I had done, he said I was the only man in the world that could have done it, I told him says I you may not be satisfied yet I told him I had paid sixty dollars to the Lawyers twenty dollars a piece, for I gave the first Lawyer I went to see just the same as I did the other two he said he did not care if I had given them five hundred a piece, so we took the cheque and over to the Franklin bank and deposited it, and I went on collecting untill they failed, I went at various business and finally went in old work business of repairing vesselles in E. B. I owend somewhat in navagation I had an interest in four three masted schooners and there was a Capt. Nickerson that wanted me to take an interest in another one she was called the Belle Halladay she was a three masted schooner and I took a 32 of her and she was a very fine sailing vesselle she was

quite old after he had been in her about a year
he got run into, and we had to repair her and I
took charge of the work, and had her repaired in
first class shape so that she rated A1. for five
years and the Captain he got very important and
began to put on quite a lot of airs I told him that
he would have to come down for I would not put up
with any of his impudence, that seemed to make him
worse and he was going to take charge of the work
himself, went to ordering the men what to do
I told the men not to take any notice of him
that I would tell them what to do right before
him, so he ordered me off the vessel, said if
I did not go he would put me off it was quite
early in the forenoon I told him if he thought
of doing it he had better commence for it
would take him all the balance of the day,
for to do it so he came up and caught hold of
me and I salloped him on the seaking and
thumped his head against the casing and I
dont know what I would have done to him,
if the carpenters had not interfered and took me
off him, he got up and went ashore himself

and I finished up the vesselle, and he whent to sea
he had some repairs done on her when he got run
into in Chestie Penselvenia and I wanted to see the
bills he whent away without giving them to me.
that winter he hauled her up in Bristol R. I.
for about three months and the next spring when he
came back to Boston, I told him I wanted to see
the bills he said I could not and he would not
show them to me and I took a Laywer with me
and demanded the bills he ordered the Laywer out
of the Cabin I told the Laywer it is all right
you come out I got out a warrent for him to have
him arrested he skulked around all day I could
not find him any whare and just at night I
had the Officer with me I got on the track of
him I found him on Comercial St. in Mr
Burses store the Officer arrested him and wanted
to know what he was going to do the Officer said it
is up to you says I wont do anything the Officer
said then you will go to Charles St. Jail
with me and he arresseted him and he showed
fight the Officer called on a Captian to help
him wanted to know if this Capt was going

back on him the Capt. told him he was not going
to lay himself liable that he was called on and he
should do his duty the Officer had his hand cuffs
to put on him and he weakened and wanted to know
what he could do the sheriff told him he could
have a chance to get a Lawyer if he wanted to he
was not there to advise him, he wanted to know
if he could go and get one, he told him no but
he could send for one so he got a man to go and
engage a Lawyer when the Lawyer came he told
him he would have to give bonds or go to Jail,
so while the man was after the Lawyer there
was 3 or 4 Capts. in the store that I was aquainted
with and we had a general shaking hands and talked
the matter over, I told them what the trouble was
they said why he is a fool and some of them even
told him so right to his head, and when the
Lawyer came the sheriff fixed his bonds to
appear the next day in court and the next day
the case was put over for four weeks and at the
end of that time he produced the bills and he
had used most five hundred dollars of the
vessells money, and I found as he was Capt.

of the vesselle and part owner that I was a partener
and I could not sue him for my part of the money
so I had to carry in a court of equeity and that would
eat my part of the vessele up so I had to give that
up and he went another trip and thought he had
the best of me so I see a fieend of mine a Mr D. C.
Mays and he advised me to go and see a commercial
Laywer John. C. Dodge, and get advise and I laid
my case befoe him he advised me not to go in
a court of equeity but told me of a new law
that had been enacted about nine years ago
that very few commercial men knew any thing
about, he said that I could liball the vesselle
for one three or five years and if she was lost
during that time or damaged in any way that the
rest of the owners would be responible for it I would
have to get three carpenters to apprise her to see
what she was worth and I — the rest of the owners
would have to pay me what she was appised at
if she was lost at the end of five years and I told
one of the owners what I was going to do he told to
wait a couple of houes and he would see I told
him I would not wait an hour I was in E. B.

at the time he wanted time to go over on commercial
St, to John Snells the agent I told him to hurry up
the past owner's name was James Menrow, and he
got back in about an hour wanted to know what I
would take for my part I figured up what I had
paid out on her and charged 6 per cent for the
money and told him what he could have my part
for, he told me to make out a bill of sale and he
would pay my part so I whent to my Laywers office
and gave him a bill of sale and he paid me my
money that ended that investement very favouable
for me I had some money on hand I did not want
to invest any more in navagation, and I talked with
my wife she said I had better get rid of navagation
and go in realestate buisness, but by the way I owned
in another three masted vessele called the William
H. White that my brother in law was in Capt
George. B. Ames and he had got in to New York and
was sick and sent for me to come on to look after
her for he had to go to the hospitial so I whent
on to N. Y. and discharged her and stayed with him
untill he got well, while I was there I sold my
part of her which was 32 share,

and got my money for her just what she cost me and the
interest, while I was there I sold a 1/16 of another 3 masted
schooner that I owned and got my money for it and when
I got home I told my wife I had sold all out but
the one she owned a sixteenth in she wanted me to sell
her I could not get any thing near what she was worth
I told her she better keep it, she thought I better
go down on the cape to a place called Onset that
was spiritual camp meeting ground and buy a
lot of land and build a house, so I did and that
was in December of 1883, and in June the first day I
moved down there that was the next year 1884, and I
fixed up my place and went to carpenting I staid there
a year that winter I run a lumber yard for a Mr
Griffin and the next spring there was a company got
a charter to build a horse railroad from East
Wareham to Onset, and they wanted me to take
stock in the company, they would give me
carpenter work to do and they wanted me for one
of the directors, and I took one share, and paid
$55.00 at the time I took it but when the cars got
running I was to pay $45.00 a hundred dollars a share
with the understanding that I might take 3 more shares

and they went on and orgisered got me to make out a
sheducal of what lumber and railroad ties they wanted
they held a meeting and chose their Presdient, and they
never notified me they let the work all out the vice
presdient got the carpenter woke, and never let me
know any thing what was going on and the Predestient
had mad all the talk with me whos name was J.C
Griffise he skulked around and I could not get any
information any way, but I found out what they
had done by an outsider and I asked some of
them they did not seem to know any thing about
what was going on, I told them you was to the
meeting wasent you they said yes and yet you
dont know any thing about what was going on, that
afternoon I was in a store and Griffise came in
when he saw me he seemed to be quite epicetid and
he began to inquire of me about the lumber says I
what do you think I know about it you got me to make
out a list of everything and did not even notify me
to attend the meeting he said there must have
been a mistake I must have been overlooked,
I told him you are a liar for it was all done
inteninolichly, he said I was a different man

from what he thought, I told him I suppose you
thought I was a fool and I thought you was a truthful
man now you have found out I am not a fool and I
have found out you are a d—m liar, he started off if
told in a little while he came back and said it was
all a mistake and he would call another meeting and
revoke the other one as soon as one of the directors
got back and I waited he did not do as he agreed
to do I got a letter in the mean time from E. B. that
Mr Kelly wanted me to come up and work for him
on vessels so I came up to E. B. and went to work
was up here about a year I made a fine years
work and my wife was with me part of the time in
E. B. and the next may I went back to Onset and
the road had been running about a year and the
stockholders had got 2 per ct of their money, but
previous to that I had sold my share out for
ten dollars which I had paid $55.00 for and the
man that I sold to paid the other forty-five and
I told him I had got more out of it than he
would ever get and he never got another cent,
and the next year when I went back from E. B.
I put a team and coach on and run

in opposition to the road, by the way there was a
man the year before put a choach on and they
run him off in about a month and a half, the
President of the road said he would run me
off in twenty days, the first trip I made to the depo
to East Wareom I took up nine passangers, and took
them away from the horse railroad depo the
President of the road was right there he told them
to wait the horse cars was coming right along they
told him to go to H—l, and horse cars got him I
got as many as could hang on my choach coming
back there was 17 in all, and I got 13 trunks and that
almost broke the Presidents heart then come the
tug of war, and the President took every measure
he could to injure me and every thing went again
him, he went to Middleborough and got a worthless
fellow by the name of Jim Burgess and he went
to interfiering with my buisness, and I booted
him about three hundred yards, that took one about
8,85.00 but I got clear of him and everybody else
did down there they offered to pay the expenses
but I would not let them so I told the horse
railroad hands to attend to their buisness

or I would serve them just as I did Burgess, and I had no more trouble with them. Then the President went to the superintent of the old Conoly road and wanted him to drive me away from the depo and he told him it was a public place, I had a right to come there, then he went to the depo master got him to order me away from the depo he said if I did not go he would drive my teams away, I told him he better send for an undertaker before he undertook that and he bustled up to me, and I went for and he went for his Office and locked himself in. There happened to be a man that the was had sent down in the Office at the time t invegstate what was going on I did not know him neither did the agent he came out and talked with me, and talked with others and went off I did not know who he was the next day he came back with another depo master and told that one his service was not needed any longer and he left, and things went along quite smoothly, untill they got a bully on the horse cars as they supposed, but when he found out what he had to contend with, he would not go to work, he went away and previous to that the

Superteint had bought a peice of land, longside
of the railroad and got a deed and the fellow that
deeded it to him did not own the land, his name
was Martin that sold the land to the road, and
before he sold it to the road he had sold it to
a widow lady and deeded it to her, he told the
lady after he deeded it to her that he could get
twenty dollars for and he would give her fifteen
instead the railroad gave him $45.00 and he
gave her fifteen and kept thirty and she gave him
a mortage back for a hundred and seventy one
dollars for a year, when the mortatage came due
she could not get the money any where without
paying 25 per ct, and I told her she should not
pay 25 per ct, and in the mean time I had been
to Plymouth and looked the tital up, and I found
that this Martin had sold this peice of land to
the railroad and given them a deed of it himself
and had moved away to Conneutte, so I told Mrs
Hammond what he had done I told I will settle
that mortage matter up, when it came due,
this Martin came about ½ past 8 Oclock one
Saturday night and I had got a warrent out for

him and had the Officer all ready, when he came
in to the notary publics Office Mrs Hammond notified
me and I went in the Office soon as Martin saw me
he seemed excited, I asked him if he had the
Mortage he said he had I asked the notary public
if he had the discharge made out for the Mortage he
said he had, I took out my pocket book I told
him to sighn the dischage and he did then I
began to read the writ-act to him, I told her
what he had done and whare he was I said you came
late to night-because it was Saturday night-
now says I, I have an Officer and a warrent all
ready to have you arrested, and says I, I have
got just $150.00 to give you and he could not see
how ttd was I says I know you cant but it is a
state prison offence and you cant get out of it.
Mrs Hammond called me in another room and
wanted to give him a hundred dollars and I
told her I would not do it says I will give him
$75.00, so she said all right-so I went back and
told him I would give him $75.00 as Mrs Hammond
wanted me to and he took the money and gave
her the Mortage, and the dischage.

and I told him to get out of the place, just as quick
as he could for if it was not for his family I would
have him arrested anyway, and he got, and I dont
think he has ever been seen there since. And I told
Mr Taylor the superteendent of that division that he had
no title to that land, he bought of Martin and
I told him the circumstances and I told him that
I would fix it for him if he wanted me to, if
not he would have to take down his fence
and I told him I would see Mrs Hammond
and get a deed from her for him or for the
railroad and he told me to go a head he would
pay me, and I did and I showed him the deed and
he said that was sasificatory and wanted to know
how much my bill was, I told him I wanted
a place to stand two teams at the depot pletform
he said I could have it, and he took a piece of
red chalk and marked out where I could have
my stand and that almost broke the Prestdent
theart of the horse railroad, and other teams would
get in my place I would order them out they bucked
against it quite hard, but the new depo master
became a partticular friend of mine.

and told them to get out—and keep out—and they
did so I had no more trouble, and every thing went
smoothly the rest—of the time that I run to the depo.
during the time that—I was running to the depo.
I sold out—twice and both parties failed and I
had to put—teams on again for the public
demanded it, the first—time I sold to a man by
the name Medekif he proved to be a most—
misterious villain and the public would not—
partinise him, so I put—on teams again got up
a good buisness and two years after I sold out again
to a man by the name of Crowell and the paid me
part—down and gave me a mortagage on the teams
for the balance and they run one summer theyfailed
I had to take the teams back, and start the buiness
again Crowell took a partener in with him
by the name of Frank Harrison—and he took the
property when the notes came due put—them in
a building and locked them up and would not—
give them up and he difyed me to get—them
finicly I had him arrested and locked up and
I had him indited, but—it never went anyfurther
I got—my teams back and I run the buiness

untill I run the horse car railroad all out, they sold out to a trolly company and I took my teams off and retired from that business on account of old age, but previous to my retirement, I dabbled somewhat in real estate, I bought one piece of land and improved it, and when I sold it I got thirteen hundred and fifty dollars for it, I had taken enough of it to pay the priciple and interest and taxes so that it only stood me two dollars, and a fellow paid me four hundred and fifty dollars down I took a mortagage for the balance, and he had it two years unfortunatly he got drunk and laid out and froze his feet and had to have them amutated and died, his name was Edward H. Gulliver and I had to foreclose, I sold it to his brother he bid it in, and paid two hundred dollars more and he failed to meet his notes and after two years I had to foreclose again and a Mr Yarinell bid it in and paid me two hundred dollars, and gave Mr. George. M. Rorter a mortagage eleven hundred and fifty dollars which Mr Rorter hold at this time, Mr Rorter was my Partener in the real estate business, and after I

lost my wife Mr Porter and I disolved
partnerships and he took the real estate and I
settled up every thing and came to E. B. again, I
stayed about one year in E. B. I was taken sick
and I went over to Somerville to board with my
wife's Nephew James. A. Russ, I stayed there about
two years then I came back to E. B. and I have
been here just one year to day. Some instances in
my life while I was in California in the butchui
buisness in the market there was a couple of men
got on a spree and they was in liquor they wanted
one of my horses to go of on a berder I would not
let him have it they was going to take it any
way I had my rifel all loaded to kill a beef
when they went to take the horse I told them to
put the horse back in the stable they would
not do it I brought my rifel up to my shoulder
they let go the horse and started for the house
there was a large fireplace in the barroom and
there was a diggerindian crouched in the corner
clost to the fire and one of them he shot the
poor fellow for no cause whatever, and the boy
they arrested him right away, and killed

a drum head court martial and took him out and
hung him to an oak tree, while they was a hanging
him I was killing a beef, I would not take any
part in it; the other fellow sobered up and kept
out of the way untill the epitement was over, I
had a young digger indian that worked for me
which I called Dick, I fed and clothed him
had a good place for him to sleep, the poor fellow
got sick, there was a carpenter's bench in the
back part of the house, on
and Dick was laying on it and one of the men
came in the shop and told me I better go out
and see they thought he was dead, I went out
to see, and sure enough the poor fellow was dead,
and I had a box made put him in and gave him
a decent burille and several of the digger indians
was there when he was buried, and they said
broch wayno (poor Dick) wayno meant broch
good, after Dick died I was coming over the
mountian with a drove of cattle in a snow storm
I had nine wild steers and I drove them as
far as they would go they began to wander of
the trail, I made up my mind to leve

them I started on and they trailed right along
after me about 2 Oclock A. M. I got over the
mountian got down the slope of the mountian
whare the snow was about 8 inches deep I came to
a place under a large fir tree and there was bare
ground for about ten feet all around the tree
when the cattle saw itd they made a dip for it and
laid down I had a box of matches in my pocket
and I built up a fire with what I could pick up
by the way I had a candel so I cut it in two and
lit one half of it there was an old windfall of
a tree close by, I broke of limbs and made quite a
comfatable fire, dryed myself as well as I could
and laid down back to the fire and fell asleep
my coat tail caught fire, I heard a voice call
brock, I jumped up and the tail of my coat was
all burnt of, it was growing daylight and I
started the cattle along the side of the mountian
untill I struck the trail again, I distinctly
recognised the voice thd spoke to me as the
boy Dick thd had died and three years
after itd, I was to a spiritual circul in
Belfast Maine and the boy Dick came

through the medium and talked digger language
and I talked with him, he said he spoke to me
when my coat was a fire, and the medium
could not speak a word of digger language, and
had never seen one and never had been to
California, the medium's name was B. H.
Colson, Now one singular instance when I was
following the sea I was bound from Boston to
Mantansa Cuba I was crossing Behamaha bank
and I over took a barque just before night the Capt,
spoke me wanted to know if I would not put a
lanter in my missinpeak so he could follow
one and I did and shortened sail so he could
keep in company and the wind being well,
to the eastered with a good full I kept on my
course suppossing I was far enough to the
eastered to chear the salt keys the weather
was thick I was 35 miles further to the westward
than I had made caculations, I whent below and
took of my oil clothes to lay down, and I heard
a voice say, go on deck and anchor, I whent up
on deck to inquire if any one had said any of
the kind, and the Mate said he had not

heard any thing of the kind, so I went below
again just as I got in the cabin I heard the
voice say again go on deck and anchor a little louder
than the first time, I went on deck to invesigat
and no one had any sound like that and I went
below again and just as I got in the cabin
I heard the voice ring out louder still go
on deck and anchor, I thought it was my Father
voice, he was an old seafaring man, but
he was over thirteen hundred miles from where
I was at that time. I went up on deck and told
the mate to get ready to wearship that I was
going to anchor, and I told the man to the
wheel to hard up and I wore ship and let
go the big anchor and the barque that was
following me, she rounded under my stearn
and done the same thing and there was considerab
swell going at the time, I was drawing fifteen feet
of water, and I thought I felt her take the ground
I asked the mate if he did and he said he
thought he did I told him to throw the lead
on the port side he reported there was three
fathoms and a half of water, I told him to

throw it on the starboard side, and he reported
nine fathoms, I told him to throw it on the port
side again, and he reported 3½ fathoms again
I told him to put the forestaysail and spanker
on her and I put a man to the wheel and told
him to keep her east-south by east, and I staid
there untill daylight and I waited for it to
clear up and when the mist cleared away, and
I could see where I was I found I was right
on the edge of the banks little salt-keys
was all in sight, when I anchored I was
running for the keys just as straight as I
could and would struck them in less than 3½
of an hour, the wind and set me 25 miles to
the west than I had reckoned, when I got
in to Mantansas Cuba, I wrote to my Father
who was living in Searsport Maine to find out
if any thing was the matter, and to write to me at
New Orleans that was the next port I was going to,
when I got in New Orleans, I got a letter from home
that they where all well, and I took a cargo of
sugarhouse molasses to New Orleans, and I load
with sugar and molasess for New York

when I got in to New York we sold the vessel and I went home, I went to see Father I asked him what time he generally went to bed, I asked him if he dreamed any thing about me that might td he could recollect, and before he had time to tell me, Mother spoke up and said yes she heard him say go on deck and anchor but as he was an old seafareing man, she took no notice of it but he said he dreamed seeing me running right straight for land, I was one time laying in Boston and freights was very dull and there was two cargoes of ice that wanted to ship one was for Willington South Colironia the other for New Orleans my vessel carried about seven hundred tons, we was talking the matter over in the commission merchants Office on Comercial St. Blanchered & Shermans, and I got up and went out took a stroll around and went up on Grays wharf I saw a man there wanted to know what vessell I was in I told him, wanted to know if I wanted to take a cargo of ice said he had two cargo's one for New Orleans and one for Willington South Caliornia, I asked him what the freight was and he told me I told him to put on a

quater of a dollar more a ton and I would take it to New
Orleans, and he wanted to know how long it would
take me to get my vesselle in to Guford's wharf
Charlstown I told him about an hour, he told
me to haul in and at 1. Oclock ttd afternoon I was
takeing in ice, I engaged the stevadore and he did
not stow it to suit me, he said if I know more
about stowing ice than he did to do it myself
I told him to go ashore and he went up town
and sued me and put a keeper aboard the vessell
for a half days work for him and his gang, I
see a Leaywer he wanted to know if he had
presented the bill, I told him he had not,
well says he we will take care of ttd I told him I
would be loaded the next day, and he said he
would see the judge, he notified this fellow
Laywer to appear the next day at 10 Oclock and I
went up with my Mate and stweard who heard
the conversation, this fellow told his story my
Laywer asked him a few questions, the judge told
the clerk to dismiss the case, I gave my Lawyer
two dollars and the fellow had to pay about
fifteen dollars, I took a green crew went into

the hole myself and stowed the cargo and I went
out of Boston in company with a square rigged brig
he asked me if I was going to keep up under the
western shore I told him no I was going to keep
out to get the wind to the eastered, he said he
was going to keep to westward for the wind would
be of shore that night just about dark I saw
a bank rising in the southwest, I kept of as
far as I could get the wind hauled around to
the southerd I kept of about 1 Oclock that
night the wind chopped in to the north east
and began to snow and I pointed my vesselle
for the shouth challen and I run out of the snow
storm, I kept along on the edge of the gulfstream
I had a very pleasant passage down to New Orlean
of eleven days, and I discharged there and loaded
with shucks and hogsteads for Cardines Cuba,
and I met that brig at Belessles at the mouth of the
missippisie, just going up the river, and I loaded
in Cardines Cuba with Molasses for Harva France
and I went from Harva France to New York. when
I got in New York the owners had sold that
vesselle had another new one all ready for me

I will now state some of my proceedings for the town of Wareham, when I was on the committee looking after the way the money had been laid out on the highways. Ques. by. H. to John C. Leary
Do you know any thing about the dirt that was taken out of the bank and hauled away and got down and then had to be hauled back again to grade? Ans. some of the dirt was mooved towards Onset bridge and used in construction of state road shulders. Quest. by. H. Do you know any thing about dirt hauled back there again Ans. no Sir. Ques. by. H. about how many loads did you haul in a day from the top of the hill say average about 900 yds. twentyfive loads a day. Ques. by. H. we have nothing to do with breaking of stone Ques. by. H. what would be the period of the time that your team would stand there while you worked on the rocks. Ans by. L. sometimes ten minuts and sometimes three hours if I got foul of a stone that weighed two or three ton we had to cut it in two take a tabele and hurkl it out before we could use the team to cart it too the crusher, then we had to use the team for filling the hole, Ques. H. you say from ten minuts to three hours which would be its

most ten minutes or three hours? ans L. three hours
the most time would average three hours. Ques. by H.
would it not have been very proper to have had some
men put on there before the team was sent there and
blasted the stone and got it all ready to roll out
before the team went there would it not have
saved the town considerable? Ans. This horse we
kept there for pulling stone out we had to have a horse
there all the time it paid better than a man would
have on the work. Ques. by H. how much an hour
did you get for your horse? Ans. three dollars a day
for self and horse. Ques. by H. how long did you
work there? about how many days.?
Ans. I would not find book. it amounted to some
where from $.40 to $.60. I think at that time it amounts
to something like $.5.0. Selectmen wanted it done for
$.5.0. Ques. by H. did you make out bill and
present it? Ans. Yes Sir.
Ques. by H: to Aruther Martin What did you see
in regard to the way work was done on our State
highway on Swift's Hill? Ans. It seems to me
that what I saw, there where some of the men that
where doing some work and some where not doing

anything. some would do more than others. There
was a certain one who dident do a great deal all the
time he was there and that was Ed. Haskins.
Ques. by. H. can you tell how many there where
at work any time when you passed there? Ans.
the last time I whent past there when they where
doing any thing. George Howes was working with Ed.
Haskins and I said to George Howes, how long befor
you will get through he said most any time, if I
can find anything else to do. Ques. by. H. was the
team doing any thing? Ans. the team was not doing
any. Ques. by. H. Mr Martien will you please state
how many loads after the stone was broken and
ready handle, you would cart in a day? Ans.
about thirty loads a day. Ques by H. did you ever
see Haskins doing any thing? Ans. yes I have
seen him working. sometimes it did not amount to
much. Ques. by H. what portion of the time
did you think you saw him working?
Ques. by. H. how many men were there when you
saw Haskins standing? Ans. I think Ed Haskins
pretended to be boss all the time he was on the
road Ques. by H. dident do any thing?

Ans. sometimes he would do a little. Ques. by. H. In the best of your judment, do you think th'd John M. Besse did his duty as a boss or was competant for a boss? Ans. no Sir. Ques. by H. of Mr Martin, do you know Mr. Martin who put Mr. Haskins in charge there, I do not know.

Ques. by. H. you know it was moved on and off again? Ans. yes Sir. Ques. by. H. who employed you? Ans. I was employed by Max. to cart stone to the crusher, then Mr Besse gave me work on the road. Ques. by. H. and Mr. Besse appeared to be boss? ans. yes he was boss on the road and Mr Savery was boss at the crusher.

Ques. by. H. Mr Snow, did ever see Haskins to work. ans. no I did not. Ques. by. H. do you consider he was doing the town justice. Ans. I know he was not. Ques. by. H. do you consider th'd the men were doing their duty as laborers when you passed? Ans. I do not. Ques by H. where they at work? ans. well I saw men at work and is pretending to work. ques. by. H. were they at work? Ans. they were not doing what I consider a mans work. Ques by. H. did you make a bargain

will Mr Beese or who you got the brick from
did they make any bargin or statement that they
would employ you to do the work? ans. sure, he
told me I should build the catch basins.
Ques. by. H. did you make any estimate of
what catch basins would cost? Ans. yes I did.
Ques. by. H. did you state it to them? ans no I
did not. Ques. by. H. will you please state about
it would cost to build those basins out-side of the
brick? Ans. the labor I should judge would be
$.25. The work was carried on in about that sort
of a way, the invesgation proved that the men
only worked about one third of the time;
Ques. by. H. to Capt. B. H. Gibbs. Dident you or your boar
make a contract to harden that road from the
cemetery to the blacksmith shop, by your house an
Capt. Nathan Gibbs and Capt. James Burgess?
Ans. yes. by contract with Thomas Gault.
Capt. H. did you make a contract with them
to have that hardening all screened before
it was put on the road? Ans. I cant
answer that without iviminating myself and I
am not obliged to do that.

Ques. by Capt. H. was it not your duty to look after
it and see that that hardening was screened
befor it was put on the road? Ques. by Capt. H.
If you made that contract to put harding on the
road, was it not your duty to see to it that
contract was properly carried out? Ques. by H.
To Charles Bryant. you have raked the stone out of
highway between the cemetary and the blacksmith
shop at East Wareham? Ans. yes. Ques. by H.
About what did it cost you? and how long were
you raking the stone? Ans. I cannot recall years
before this. I would not dare say. Ques. by H.
did it take you any longer than it did last
year? Ans. no Sir. Ques. by H. what did it
cost last year? Ans. about $15.00 Hacker's
bill was $61.50 cts. for one year. while Bryant
did it for $15.00 a year for two years before Hacker's
did it.

one instance in my life, when I was following the
sea I was Mate with a Capt: that never had a Mate
that he spoke well off, and he wanted me to go to
the Westindies with him as Mate, he was a particular
friend of mine and I told him that if I went
with him it would break up our friendship
he wanted to know why? I told him because
he never had a man that suited him; well
he said I would so I shipped with him and as
soon as we left the warf, I went foward to
clearing up and getting ready to cockbill the
anchors that was have them all ready to let go
if need be, it was what all vessels does untill
they get out to sea, and the Capt: came foward
and began to give orders, I went aft on the
quater he discovered that I had gone away and
he came aft wanted to know why I was not
attending to my duty? and I told him I
shipped to take charge of one end of that vessell
and if he wanted the foward end I would
take the after end, and we read the riot
act over to each other, he said it was
munity I told the man to the wheel

to put it up and let her wabel around. He
ordered the man to keep her on her course, and
after we had a loud talk he told me if I
would take the forward end he would keep
the after end, I told him all right, and I
never went with a better man, than he was
but he kept his place and I kept mine. and
when I got back they asked him how he got
along with me he said first rate he never
had a better man, and they wanted to know how
I got along with him I told them allright, they
said you had trouble with him before you got out
of the harbour, I told them that was all the trouble
I had while I was with him; when we was in
Cardines Cuba, the men wanted liberty to go ashore
he said that would not do for they would leave
I told him I would be resposible for the men,
well he said they might go I told him they
five dollars a peice Oh no I told him I would let
them have the money if he did not have it, if
he would be responsible, well he said he would,
let them have the money and the men went ashore
I told them it they got drunk not to come

aboard but to stay untill they got sober, and the next morning, they was all back and ready to go to work expept one and about three Oclock in the afternoon he came down to the shore and hailed the vessell, I sent the second mate and two men ashore after him when he came aboard he was so drunk he could hadly stand when he came aboard he backed up against the rail said he was all ready to go to work, I told him he better go to the focastel and I would call him when I wanted him, I did not see any thing more of him untill the next morning, the Capts wife went ashore on Sunday and after he went ashore I left the vessell in charge of the second Officer and I went ashore I was sitting down on a verander of the second floor with some Mates talking with them my Capt was in a similer place right opposite with some other Capts and our crew and a lot of other sailors they got fighting in the street right underneath of us, my Capt spoke across the street and said Mr Hanning our men is fighting down there I told him let them fight, he and the other Capts went down, my Capt got his

lip cut, one the other Capts got his arm broke
and I sat calmly looking on, Another incident in my
life. One time in the city of Bangor when I was a
young man, I was boarding in a house where there
were the man of the house was pretty wild sort
of chap his name Bryant, they was having a
revival meeting in the Methodstist Church and
Bryant had got converted I did not know it
he wanted me to go to Church one Evening, and
just before the meeting was closed the minister
came to me a big bully Minister and wanted
to know if I had religion I told I had wanted
to know how long I had experienced religion
I told him I always had, he wanted to know
what it consisted of, I told him to do as near
right as I possible could, wanted to know if
I had ever made an open confession, I told
him I had not made any more than living a
moral life, he wanted to know if I thought that
sufficent to save me, I told him I did, and he
wanted to know if I wanted them to pray for
me, I told him I had no objections to pray
for me but I just as life ask any to eat for me

as to pray for me, asked me if I did not believe in prayer, I told him I did, that every desire of the heart was a prayer, well says he thank God and he went in the pulpit and he raked me for and aft, then there was another old fellow got up and gave me a broadside, I told them I did not come there to be abused and I considered them both backards and fagabonds and if they made any more that kind of talk there would be a scenen right there in the church so I got up and walked out, they closed the meeting I went to my boarding house, and when the man came home I went for him I asked him if I did any thing to disturb the meeting he said no, the next day when I went to dinner one of the members of the church a woman that had not the most savoring chachecter, when I came in she made the expersion there comes that weretch it did not take me but a minute to open on her, and she got out of the way just about as quick as she could and it pleased the landlady where I boarded, and the next day it was a

stormy day it was snowing and sleeting, and I
happend to meet the Minister on the sidewalk
I went for him and was going to thrach him
so he pulled of his coat threw it on a picket
fence, and said he was commanded to fight
the devil wharever he met him, and I began
to survay him I worked around him and told
him to go to H— and walked off, and I always
considered about the smartest thing I ever done
for he was one of the most powerful men that
was in the state of Maine, I found out after, and
if he had got hold of me I think he would
have wiped up some of the snow with me,
and the other Ministers in the city got hold of the
contervery we had the Baptist Minister and the
Congergational Minister and the Universal
Minister they came all three of them to see me
and I told them just what was said and what
I said and I could prove it, and they wanted
to know if I was Capt Hanning's son I told them
I was I supposed, well they said your Father is
a Methodist Minister, I said he was, and
then Tilltion the Minister std I had the

controversity with found who I was and who my
Father was, those Ministers and the Churches they
told him that he must apoglise or it would
be carried in court and he did not loose any time
in apoligising, and I told him I would accept
it after quite a persuasion by the other Ministers,
but I had no apoligy to make to him, and that
settled the matter, This all took place when I was
a young man, shortly after that I was married to my
first wife, a year or two after I was married I
built a house in Belfast a year or so after my
house was built, the Campmeeting grounds was
in Northport Maine about 4 miles from Belfast.
While they was holding their meetings my Father
brought this same minister Mr Tillison by name
to my house and stayed all night, but he made
no reference to the trouble we had previous to that
and that was the last I ever saw of him, but
while I was in the army his sister was an
army nurse and she nursed me when I was
sick with the typhoid fever I was at that
time at Fort Sckyler Long Island sound New york

when I got over the fever, I got a furlough for
thirty days to go home to Belfast to see my
children, when my furlou was up I went back
to fort skyler and went from there to the front
to join my regiment. I got back Saturday
night to my regiment and monday morning we
had marching orders, and about 1 Oclock we
attacked the rebles at Kellysford on the
Reappanaka River and we took about three
hundred and fifty prisoners the next day we
had another fight at Brandy station and we
drove the rebels out of their winter quaters, the
army of the Potomac went in the winter quaters
ourselves after we got settled down for winter
the inspecting officer inspected our Bregrade
and reported it the dirtest Bregrade in the
army of the Potomac and our regement the
4 maine was reported to be the dirtest
regement there was in the Bregrade, the
inpecting officer said there was only one
man that was fit to go on inspection
and that was Sargent Hanning of Co K.

the orderly Sargent of Co. K. got a promotion
promotion to second leutient but there
was not men enough in the Company to
muster him, and Sargent Nickerson
was acting orderly, and they ordered
Sargent Drake He had been orderly
to take the Company again, he did not
want to do it because he expected to
get mustered, so they ordered Hanning to
take the Company and I would not do it
without an orderlys warrent, and the Konel
came to me and told me to take the Company
I told him I would when I had a warrent, he
said if I did not he would put me in the
ranks. I told him to go ahead and General
Ward told the Captian to give me an
Orderlys warrent and next day in the afternoon
we went on Bregrade drill and when we
went in to Camp, I found a large envelope
on my bed I opend it there was a warrent
when the revelee beat for dress prade I
went out and ordered the Company to fall
in but they did not obey at once I spoke

sharfly and they began to fall in, and
Sargent Nickerson wanted to know what
thd meant, I told him to take his place
in the rear of the company; but he kept
on talking I told him to take his
place or I would put him under arrest
so then he took his place, We whent dressprade
and when the Orderlys came to the center and
reported I was the left company I told the
Adjudgent I had no report to make, he said
all right and next morning at roll call
Sargent Nickerson wanted to know what it meant
I told him to go to the Captian, and I asked
two days to clean the company up the Adjudgen
reported in about half an hour thd I could
have it and more if I wanted it so I whent to
work making prepations for soap and water
and large Camp kettles and I got the men
to work cleaning up, I had them all at work
cleaing up the company grounds getting readi
to wash up, I taked with Capt. Ash General
Ward's Ade what I shoud do with Doake
for he had been promoted to Second Leetuient

he said he had his choice to take the company
or go back to the fourth Sargent so he went
back to fourth Sargent, but still was
acting Leetuente Capt. Nash said trot him
out and clean him up for he was as dirty
as any of the rest. So I sent a corporal to
him to come out and clean up he sent
word back to tell the Orderly to go to Hell
I steped over to head quarters and reported
to Capt. Nash what he said, he was the
Generals ADC, he told me to trot him out
I sent a corporal and two Privates to bring
him up to the guard tent and to bring him
if they had to drag him all the way as I was
responsible. One of the Privates came back and
said he would not and the Captain he came
up rageing. I said Capt. I have no
judesrsction over you but I'll report you
so he went to Captain Leibby a friend of mine
and he told him the Circumstances the
Adjotugent was present, they to him to
come to me and apolgize and he could
not do it any to quick so he did

and he told Doak he would have to go and clean up, he said he would if I would call the guard away, so I sent to Captian Nash to know what I could do. he came over to the guard house and Doak was standing there under guard and Capt Nash told him he would have to go in the guard house under guard and be courtmartialed, for disobaing his supiour and I laid the case before General Ward and I beged for mercy for him, General Ward whent over with me to the guard tent and repermanded him and told him to go and clean up, and about every Officer in the regerment came to my tent and had a Jublee. so Saturday afternoon when we whent on inspection Capt Nash reported the 4 Maine regerment was the cleanest regerment in the Bergrade and Company K. was the cleanes Company in the regement with the exception of one man and thd was Sargent Nickerson. I told Sargent Nickerson to ——— himself up to be ready to go on inspection Sunday morning and he was

I had no more trouble with any of them.
The Capt. he would give the men orders to get liquor
and make trouble for me so I told him if he gave
them any more orders for liquor that I would report
him if I had to go to General Mead's head quaters
so when they went to him again for an order he told
them to come to me and get me to write it and he
would sighn it so they come and wanted me to write
an order for 2 dollars and I wrote it and they went to
settlers store and presented their order and the
suttler wanted to know what they wanted they said
a bottle of wisky he told them he could not let
them have it unless it was wrote wisky, they
came back and wanted me to write it for a bottle of
wisky I told them no Sir so they went of and
there came a very rainy day there was 2 of them
went out and got liquor somewhare and they was
making an aful sight of trouble the Captain he
came out and tried to stop them they was going
to lick him so he came in my quaters and
began to use language unbecoming of a Captain
I asked him if saw that hole I made in my
Cabin and I told him to get out of it as quick as

your ear, there was a log about six inches through
that he had to step over there was about 4 inches
of dirty muddy water running in the gutter of
the Company street he slipped and went down
on his back in the gutter and he had to roll over
to get up by that time he was about all covered
with mud then he started to the Adjudgent
to report me and have me arrested the Adjudgent
told him he would do it and my friend Libby
was in the Adjudgents Office he told the Capt
that he better not be to fast before he stated
the case for he might get into trouble, that
had the effect to bring him to his senses
Capt Libby asked him the cause of the trouble
and he said he went to order me to take care
of the men he then asked him how he approached
me, he said well I suppose I did speak a little
kind of ruff Capt Libby said now we are coming
at it what did you say to him? I asked him
what kind of a d— orderly he was and he asked
me if I saw that hole I made and told me to
get out as quick as I could and I stepped out
slipped in the ditch feel on my back and

rolled over, now Capt. Leibly said you better
and tell him to take care of those men and
he came back and said Orderly them men has got
liquor some whare and I dont know whare they have
got it I wish you would take care of them, I put
my rubber blanket over my shoulders for it was
raining very hard I went out and told them to
go into their quarters and the worst one he began
to put up a fight I caught him by the collar he
went headlong I picked him up and put him
in his quaters when I went out one of the other two was
gone I did not see him any whare neither did I
look for them, the other was standing there I
said I want you to get in your quaters for it
was damp out there and he whirled around him
arm and said Sargent get my how you for
I love you, I told him never mind he he
drank liquor and chewed tobacco and I led him
to his quaters and I told them to stay there untill
I called them I did not hear any thing from
them untill the next morning, sometime after
that there was another troublesome man got liquor and
they put him under guard he walked out by the river

and whent off, I was eating my supper they came
and told me Abe had got out and gone I told him
to go get him I told them I thought they was a smart
lot of 15 men to let one man get away so I whent up
to his Orderlys Sargents quaters he was talking pretty
loud and had been after Sargent Hanning to get
him, he says he cant me the Sargent told him
he better be careful he said I dont care about
any other man but him just as he said that I
opened the door and said Abram I want you
he came out and started to run I told him
to hault, I told the guard to fire as I said
that he dropped down on the ground and said
I would have to carry him to the guard tent
I told him to get right up he got up I took
hold of his arm and led him of to the guard
tent put him under guard again he began to
act pretty bad he got his jackknife out and
began to tell what he might do I told him to
give me the jackknife he put it in his pocket
I whent and told him to give it to he took it
right out and gave it to me, I mad up a bed
and told him to lay down and he started

to climb out of the chimney fell back and
burnt himself and burnt his clothes then I
took him put him in a place I fixed for
him and laid him down, he laid there
the balance of the night the next morning
the Letuente reported him and I reported
the Letuente he belonged to my company he
was going to take a months pay away from
him so I said it was best to have the
whole thing investagated and they let him go.
Instances of the army, When we was at Camp
at Alexanderia the first year of the war a
Sargent and Privates got drunk they whent
to the Conoale for an order to get more liquor, he
would not give it to them, he ordered them
to their quaters and they was going to clean him out
and he ordered them arrested, the Officer of the guard
sent a corporal and to privates, they picked on the
Corporal and cleaned him out the privates they run
the Conoral came to me, I was sitting in my tent
writing a letter he told me he wanted to go and
arrest Melmer and Libby, I not being on duty
I hestiated for a moment and the Conoal said

he did not ask me as an order but as a favour
and I got up put on my side arms went down to
the guard tent and got two privates marched up to
the Consals quaters told him I was ready he told me
to take them dead or alive if they showed any resistence
to shoot them right down, when I went after them they
was out on the prade ground on the right of the
rigement smashing their fist together saying what
they was going to do, when they saw me coming Sargent
Libby he slunk back in his tent Ulmer he stood
up as straight as a candel, I told the men one on each
side of him that if he showed any resistance to
shoot him right down, I told them to take him to
the guard tent and I took Sargent Libby he got
right up and locked in my arm walked of to the
guard tent with me, Sargent Libby said put us in
on the right they made a place up for them to sleep
I went to my quaters, next morning about daylight
the Consal went to the guard tent and told them
to go to their quaters after guard mounting he sent for
them and he gave them a regular repremanding
and told them and if ever they did anything of that
kind again he would punish them

he then told them to go to their quaters, after they started, he called them back and asked why they did not resist Sargent Hanning and Libby he puckered up his mouth half laughed and said he saw hell in Hannings eye and he dident in the corporal's. Previous to that we had a man in our company that chanalaged any man in the regement to warstal him wilt back holt and there was a man that exapted it and the he chanaglid throwed him three times and he gave it up. the fellow told him he admired his courage but he was a d— fool for there was not a man in the regement that could throw him I (that is Sargent Hanning) spoke up and said <u>what</u> he says yes I mean it, he says do you want to take it up, I told him I would when he said he was ready, he went on his back, says I was not ready, I told him he could try it again and he backed and filled when I got ready he came down wilt such force and I ontop of him that I had to help him up, I asked him if he was satisfied said yes, I told him there was men in this regement that would hold me out to arms length and I could not help myself.

after I was wounded and got able I was sent home to be mustered out after the expiration of my enislement, I was three years and three months in the service. The war lasted nine months after that.

At A Child's Grave.

My Friends: I know how vain it is to gild a grief with words, and yet I wish to take from every grave its fear. Here in this world, where life and death are equal kings, all should be brave enough to meet what all the dead have met. The future has been filled with fear, stained and polluted by the heartless past. From the wondrous tree of life the buds and blossoms fall with ripened fruit, and in the common bed of earth, patriarchs and babes sleep side by side. Why should we fear that which will come to all that is? We cannot tell, we do not know, which is the ~~greater~~ greater blessing—life or death. We cannot say that death is not a good. We do not know whether the grave is the end of this life, or the door of another, or whether the night here is not the somewhere else a dawn. Neither can can we tell which is the more fortunate — the child dying in its mother's arms, before its lips have learned to form a word, or he who journeys all the length of life's uneven road, painfully taking the last slow steps with staff and crutch.

Every cradle asks us "Whence?" and every coffin "Whither?" The poor barbarian, weeping above his dead, can answer these questions just as well as the robed priest of the most authentic creed. The tearful ignorance of the one, is as consoling as the learned and unmeaning words of the other. No man, standing where the horizon of a life has touched a grave, has any right to prophesy a future filled with pain and tears. May be death gives all there is of worth to life. If those we press and strain within our arms could never die, perhaps that love would wither from the earth.

may be this common fate treads
from out the paths between our
hearts the weeds of selfishness and
hate. And I had rather live and
love where death is king, than have
eternal life where love is not. Another
life is nought, unless we know and love
again the ones who love us here.

They who stand with breaking hearts around
this little grave, need have no fear. The
larger and the nobler faith in all that is,
and is to be, tells us that death, even at
its worst, is only perfect rest. We know
that thorough the common wants of
life— the needs and duties of each hour—
their grief will lessen day by day,
until at last this grave will be to them
a place of rest and peace— almost of joy.
There is for them this consolation: The dead do
not suffer. If they live again, their lives
will surely be as good as ours. We have no fear.
We are all children of the same mother, and

the same fate awaits us all. We, too, have our religion, and it is this: Help for the living—Hope for the dead.

(After spending time unlocking Charles' life, editing his autobiography, I can only assume the eulogy given by Colonel Ingersoll embodied Charles' philosophy of life and death. It was, therefore, important for Charles to end his book with the beautifully written piece given at a child's funeral.

Portland Oregon, Dec 13 1909

Dear Aggie & Janey, I recd – your
letter this morning, was sorry to hear of
your loss, wat are you going to do let
me know what you intend to do.
did you get those Notes. do you need
Money, tell me what you intend to
do, whom are you going to Like
with look out for yourselves, I will
Try and get shaitened out here & come
back as soon as I can, you have
got to have some one to look out for
you, goodby write soon
                    Your Father James Carr

153 liverpool St East Boston

March 20" 1910

Dear Grand Children I Will trie and
Write you all three in this letter you
wrote me a fine letter and I Was Pleased to
git it it was fine and I should like to
see you all and I hope that I shall I long
for Good warme Wether so that I can git out
I saw your aunt Glenn Charley last friday
and he Was the furst Grand Child that
I ever how he Was a fine looking man
I Was Promed of him I Will send you
some thing soon By Express I dont
think that I Can git to see you befor
Gone for I have bisnes to look after the
last of may and I must atende to that
my helth is quit good for an old man
I must belide that I am giting old
I Will soon bee Eightly and that
is fining am hone are Exede in
I hope that Agnes will take good
care of hear self and Nat Wowgave
hear studeys she Will git along just
as Well you Must Exense my Poor writing
for I dont write much and when I
see you all I Will tell you more
then I can Write so you Write
as oftin as you can for I like to
hear from you I git letters from
you but quit oftin she tells me
how you all are an I cant think
of eney thing more to write
so I shall hafto close
fram your Grand
Paw C E Hanning

Miss ____ A. Corr.
White River Junction, Vt

The Porter-Whidden Company,
East Boston

BOSTON
DEC 15
12-30P
19 10
MASS.

EAST BOSTON
STATION

U.S. POSTAGE

Miss Janay Carr.
White River Junction.
Vermont.

Box 419.

297 Meridian St E Boston
Dec 13 1910
Dear Children I will write
you a few lines to let you know
that I am well and I hope this will
find you the same I Gat Janays
kind letter and was glad to
hear from you all I will send
you five Dallars one fore
James and two for you and
2 for Agnis and you can
Buy samthing fore it your
selves I should like to
see you all and I hope I
shall sune I will write
to Jessie and send them
five Dallars and your ant
Ellen all so and send her the
same

I wood like to hear
let me know if you git
this letter and I will
close for this time from
your loving grandfather
A E Manning

297 Meridian St
East Boston
April 3 1910
Dear Grand child I will
anser your loving letter
after so long time But you
must Excuse me for I ha
had a bad time with my
feet I have had the chilbla
so that Mg feet was swelan
so Bad that I could not
git enny dry shoals for two
week and it taak me a about all
the time to loak after them
But tha are Better than
my helth is 2 wit well at my
Ages for an old man I have
Jest writen a letter to your
aunt Ellen I have had an letter

had ane letter from
Jessy and she sed that
tha had Jest got thare she
sed that she was not home sick
when she wrote the dear
children I hope that tha
will due well it makes
me feel lansom for to have
them go so far away
I can't think of Enny thing
more to write now so I will
clase I will write yoo
when I am coming up to se
yoo and I want yout write
soon and let me Know how yoo
all are tak of love from
your loving Grand father
C E Hanning

Miss Jane E. Carr
White River Junction
Vermont

297 Meridian St
East Boston
April 19, 1911

Dear Children Dear Jane
I got your kind letter
and was glad to hear
from you I was away
when it came and I did
not git it untell yesterday
I got that wrap that
Earnes sent me and it
was fine I will send
you a five dollar bill
and you can divide it
between you three and I
will try and come up
at the close of your
school and see you

want to see you all for I love
you and you and Charles Farley
and your aunt Ellen and all
I have just writen to Zelsea and your
aunt Ellen and this is the fifth
letter that I have writing
this morning and I amirald
as I will with lots a love
to you all and write as often
as you can I got a letter from
Zelsea and tha was well and
tha liked well so I will
close with love from
your Grand father
C E Hanning

297 Meridian St E Boston
Oct 5 1911

Dear Children I Will
Dear Janey I got your
Welcome letter and was
glad to hear from you I
am quit Well at Present
I hope this Will find you
all Well I had a letter
from your aunt Ellen and
she Was quit Well for him
I had a letter from Jessie
and she sead that tha Was all
Well and contented tha
liked acct tha she sead that
sh had Picked 170 qt of Blue
Bergs and she got 10 ct a qt
for them she sead that

charles had Plenty of
Work and tha Wore
Doing Well she head that
one of charles hordes got
a nail in his foot and he
was quit lame for a short
time bu he was almost well
I shall write to them to
Day I hope this will
find you all Well I
hope that you can git
Jennie Jordyth to keep house
for you she is real nice she
has a Plenty hard time I will
close With lots of love to you
all Write as often as you can
from your grand father
C E Hanning

GENEALOGY

CHARLES ELISHA HANNING and HANNAH FLOYD PATTERSON'S DESCENDANTS

Charles was born in Portland, Cumberland, Maine, May 25, 1830, died January 8, 1917, at the Soldier's Home in Chelsea, Massachusetts, and was buried in the Belleville Cemetery in Newburyport, Massachusetts. Grave No. 99688108. He married Hannah Floyd Patterson on April 8, 1852, in Belfast, Maine, and they had two girls, Ellen E. Hanning and Emma Aurelia Hanning. His parents were Deborah and John Hanning who lived on John's father's farm in Old Town, Penobscot, Maine. (No concrete information concerning these two has surfaced yet, except Charles' father, John, came from Prussia.)

Hannah Floyd Patterson was born April 12, 1827, died November 23, 1889, and was buried in the Grove Cemetery in Belfast, Maine. Grave No. 119717349. Hannah and Charles were divorced in 1860. Her parents were Robert Patterson the 5th and Mary Sally Polly Shute who lived in Belfast. Robert the 5th was born February 21, 1792, in Saco, Maine, and died 1879, in Salem, Maine. Polly Shute was born January 8, 1791, in Prospect, Maine, and died November 15, 1857, in Maine. Robert the 5th and Polly Shute were married in Belfast, Maine, on November 27, 1814.

CHARLES ELISHA HANNING'S, second marriage, to ROXANA WEYMOUTH

Roxana was born in August 1827, in Rye, New Hampshire, married Charles Elisha Hanning in Boston, Massachusetts, November 8, 1864, and died January 11, 1906, in Wareham, Massachusetts. She was buried in the Forest Hills Crematory in Roxbury, Massachusetts. Roxana and Charles had no children. Roxana's parents were married in Belmont, Maine, in 1828. Her father, John Weymouth, was born in 1794, in Rye, New Hampshire, died June 26, 1875, in Morrill, Waldo, Maine, and was buried in the Morrill Village Cemetery. Grave No. 47713553. Roxana's mother was Lois, aka Louise Robinson, was born December 27, 1794, in Belmont, Maine, and died November 12, 1855, in Morrilll, Waldo, Maine. She was buried in the Morrill Village Cemetery. Grave No. 47713577. John and Lois were married in 1828, in Belmont, Maine. Charles' two girls, Ellen and Emma, were Roxana's step children.

Possibly Roxanna Weymouth. This photo is very small and was probably a locket photo that Hanning took with him across the globe on his adventures.

ELLEN E. HANNING and AARON OSGOOD SWETT

Aaron Swett—seated on porch— and, left to right standing,
Ellen Hanning Swett, Fannie and Ernest Shephard.

Ellen and Aaron were married September 15, 1874, in Boston, Suffolk, Massachusetts. Ellen was born August 11, 1852, in Belfast, Maine. She died in Newburyport, Essex, Massachusetts in 1930. Aaron was born October 24, 1831, in Amesbury, Essex, Massachusetts, died September 16, 1923, in Newburyport, and was buried in the Belleville Cemetery. Grave No. 99822097. Their residence from 1880, until death was given as 289 Merrimac Street, Newburyport Ward 6, Essex, Massachusetts. Aaron and Ellen had no children. Aaron's father was Timothy Swett, born September 21, 1801, and died August 14, 1886. Aaron's mother was Polly Osgood, born September 15, 1803, and died March 26, 1870. Timothy and Polly were married in Salisbury, Massachusetts on June 24, 1827 by Reverend Benjamine Sawyer. They both died in Amesbury, Massachusetts, and were buried in the Salisbury Point Burying Ground in Amesbury.

EMMA AURELIA HANNING and ALMOND SHEPHERD

Emma Hanning was born in Belfast, Waldo County, Maine, on November 24, 1854, married Almond Shepherd late in 1872, or early in 1873, and died December 1, 1909, in Hartford, Windsor, Vermont. I assume she was buried in the Cemetery in Hartford. Almond's father was Amasa Shepherd, born July 6, 1804, in Jefferson, Lincoln, Maine, and died September 22, 1867, in Jefferson. Amasa married Alosia (or spelled) Elosia G. Arnold on March 2, 1840, in Jefferson. Elosia was born in 1815, and died March 26, 1883, in Jefferson. Elosia and Amasa Shepherd are buried in the Maine, Nathan Hale Cemetery in the Shepherd's Family section. Amasa's mother and father were Samuel Shepherd and Martha Cochran.

They were married October 11, 1797. Samuel Shepherd was born October 8, 1774, and died April 25, 1855. Martha Shepherd was born June 15, 1773, and died August 4, 1848. Elosia and Amasa had two boys, Albert Shepherd and Almond Shepherd. (NOTE: These ancestors of Almond's were found when trying to get information on Almond, so I decided to include it. For many years when relatives were together there was conversation about the fact that Almond was an adopted child from the Palmers. There is nothing I can find on Almond until the 1850 U.S. Census, when he was eight years old. His birth would then have been in 1842, five months after his brother Albert was born. It is my belief, that Almond was born July 21, 1842, into the Luther and Martha Palmer family of Georgetown, Massachusetts. The baby's birth name was Almond Palmer. Within the first month of birth, Almond was adopted by Elosia and Amasa Shepherd. The "d" at the end of Almond was not dropped until later.) Almond died January 1, 1890, in Monroe, New Hampshire, of pneumonia. He was forty-seven years old. In 1860, Almond was at home in Jefferson, Lincoln, Maine, with his family. In 1880, Almond was a farmer, married to Emma A. Hanning, and living in Monroe, Grafton, New Hampshire. Emma and Almond had three boys, George M. Shepherd, Charles H. Shepherd, and Ernest A. Shepherd.

ALBERT SHEPHERD and MARY L. GOULD

Albert Shepherd was born February 17, 1842, in Jefferson, Maine, died November 29, 1921, in Nashua, Hillsboro, New Hampshire, and was buried in the Evergreen Cemetery in Portland, Maine. Albert was in New Hampshire for only ten weeks before he died. Grave No. 128733926. Albert married Mary L. Gould, April 3, 1869, in Beddington, Washington, Maine. Albert and Mary had four children. In 1880, they lived in Monroe, Grafton, New Hampshire. In 1900, they lived in Portland City, Ward 1, Cumberland, Maine. Mary was born September 1, 1846, in Machias, Washington, Maine, died September 25, 1907, in Machias, and was buried in the Evergreen Cemetery in Portland, Maine. Grave No. 128747705. Her parents were Jacob S. Gould and Rebecca Cates, married October 5, 1844, in Beddington, Maine.

GEORGE M. SHEPHERD AND MAMIE ELIZABETH CHAMBERLAIN

George was born in Ripley, Maine, January 1, 1874. The birth was registered in the Town of South Hadley where his parents, Almond and Emma Shepherd lived. He married Mamie Elizabeth Chamberlain on January 4, 1899, in Laconia, Belknap County, New Hampshire. George died May 16, 1904, in a drowning accident while working on a log drive up in Maine. Mamie was born in Bath, New Hampshire, about 1873, and died in childbirth in Monroe, New Hampshire, on February 28, 1899. Her father's name was Gilbert Chamberlain and her mother's name was Mary Jane Bedell.

CHARLES HANNING SHEPHERD and JESSIE VERNA NOYES

Seated, Charles Hanning Shepherd. Back row, Olive Sanders holding baby girl Fay, Jessie Shepherd, Mervin Sanders holding Glenna, age two. The family celebrated Charles and Jessie's Golden Wedding Anniversary.

Charles was born in Monroe, New Hampshire, February 18, 1877, and died in Dryden, Ontario, Canada, April 1, 1955. He was buried in the Dryden Cemetery on April 4, 1955. He married Jessie Verna Noyes, November 14, 1900, in Lyman, New Hampshire. Jessie was born November 28, 1880, in Easton, Grafton, New Hampshire, and died January 10, 1956, in Dryden, Ontario. She was buried in the Dryden Cemetery. Her father's name was Henry Kimball Noyes, and her mother's name was Mary H. Little. The family emigrated to Canada, arriving in Highwater, Memphremagog, Quebec, on February 28, 1911. They settled in Barclay, on the outskirts of Dryden, Ontario, on March 2, 1911. Charles and Jessie had two children, Almon Henry Shepherd and Sybil Irene Shepherd.

ALMON HENRY SHEPHERD and EDNA PEARL CRERAR

Almon was born October 11, 1901, in Easton, New Hampshire, married Edna Pearl Crerar, February 6, 1924, and died April 11, 1972, in Dryden, Ontario. Pearl, as she was known, was born in Oxdrift, Ontario, on November 14, 1902, and died March 29, 1986, in Dryden. Pearl's father was John Anderson Crerar and her mother was Barbara Skene. Almon and Pearl are buried in the Family Plot in the Dryden Cemetery. They had four children, Marguerite Ottoline (Peggy) Shepherd, Keith Gordon Shepherd, Doreen Barbara Shepherd, and Barry Clinton Shepher

Pearl and Almon Shepherd's family. Standing: Pearl Shepherd, Almon Shepherd, Keith Gordon Shepherd. Front Row: Peggy, Barry and Doreen.

Marguerite Ottoline (Peggy) was born February 8, 1924, in Dryden, Ontario, married Francis (Frank) Reid on November 28, 1947, died June 24, 1996, at the age of seven-two. She was buried in the Dryden Cemetery after the service June 27, 1996. Peggy and her brother Keith died several hours apart at two of the hospitals in Thunder Bay. Peggy and Frank had four children and ten grandchildren.

Frank Reid and Peggy Shepherd Reid with three of their four children, Jerri, Jim, and Janice Shepherd.

Keith Gordon Shepherd was born May 22, 1927, in Fort Frances, Ontario, and died June 24, 1996, at the Port Arthur General Hospital, Ontario. He was buried June 28, 1996, in the Dryden Cemetery. Keith started work at the Dryden Paper Company in 1943, and retired in 1988. He married Kathleen (Kae) Elsie Huzzey, December 23, 1954, in Dryden. Kae and Keith had three children and four grandchildren. Kathleen was born in Stuartville, Manitoba, on November 3, 1927, and died March 8, 1986, at the Princess Margaret Hospital in Toronto, Canada. She was laid to rest on March 12, 1986, in the Dryden Cemetery. After Kathleen passed away Keith married Evelyn Skene.

Doreen Barbara Shepherd was born November 21, 1935, in Dryden, Ontario. She married James Cox, June 17, 1955, and are living in Osoyoos, B.C. Canada. They have three children. Debra Lauraine, born in Dryden, on September 26, 1956, Douglas James, born in Hamilton, Ontario, February 27, 1964, and Kevin Patrick, born in Montreal, Quebec, on August 29, 1964. The two boys were adopted at a young age.

Barry Clinton Shepherd was born September 20, 1938, in Dryden, Ontario, and married Birte (Bobbie) Schmidt on June 23, 1962. Bobbie was born February 8, 1940, in Kolding, Denmark, and immigrated to Canada with her parents in 1951. Her father, Niels, was born May 13, 1912, and died in 1982, in Dryden, Ontario. Bobbie's mother, Marie Uldall, was born September 9, 1918, and died in 1985 in Dryden. Bobbie and Barry are living in Dryden, Ontario, and have two children, five grandchildren, and three great grandchildren.

SYBIL IRENE SHEPHERD and HERMAN SANDERS

Sybil was born July 8, 1906, in Landaff, New Hampshire, died March 13, 1995, in Dryden, Ontario. Sybil and Herman Leslie Sanders were married in Thunder Bay, Ontario, May 16, 1923. Herman was born in Oshawa, Ontario, on February 5, 1901, and died September 23, 1968, in Dryden. After Herman passed away, Sybil and Hector McAllister McKay were married on December 14, 1970, in Dryden. Hector was born January 7, 1899, and died September 30, 1992. Sybil and Herman had two boys. Mervin Sanders and Almon Robert Sanders.

Mervin Sanders was born November 16, 1923, in Dryden, and died October 20, 2010, in Dryden. He married Olive Jane Ethelyne May 21, 1947, in Oxdrift, Ontario. They had five children and ten grandchildren. Olive Jane was born March 20, 1927, in Oxdrift, and died February 23, 2009, in Dryden.

Almon Robert (Bob) was born March 20, 1930, in Dryden, and died March 3, 2003. He married Dorothy June Odell, October 4, 1952, in Dryden. They had four children and seven grandchildren. Dorothy was born June 25, 1931, in Hargrave, Manitoba and is still living in Dryden.

ERNEST ALMON SHEPHARD and FANNIE ARCHER
(Note: Spelling of Shephard.)

Ernest was born July 6, 1881, in Monroe, Grafton, New Hampshire, and died January 9, 1955, of Hodgkins Disease in Hartford, Windsor, Vermont. Ernest married Fannie Lillian Archer, November 2, 1912, in Hartford. He worked for the New England Telephone Company as a lineman. Ernest and Fannie's home before moving to White River Junction in 1935, was in Hartford, Vermont. Fannie was born December 8, 1881, in Orford, Grafton, New Hampshire, and died November 7, 1957. Her Father was Josiah Archer and her mother was Mary Rebecca Hannaford. Fannie and Ernest had two girls, Emma Mae and Virginia Jane.

On the Occasion of Ernest Shephard's Funeral

Left to Right: Randy, Georgia, Betty Bailess, Charlene Wright, Virginia Wright (hidden), Ernie Pierce, Edgar Pierce, Emma Mae Pierce, Susan Bailess, Becky Pierce, Fannie Shephard, Abby (Fannie's sister), Jane Bailess and Andy Bailess. This picture was taken after Ernest Shephard's funeral.

Emma Mae was born March 31, 1918, in Hartford, Vermont, and died September 24, 1959. She married Edgar Noble Pierce, November 2, 1937. Edgar was born April 4, 1913, in Hartford, Windsor, Vermont, and died September 25, 1992, in Thetford Center, Orange County, Vermont. June 16, 1973, Edgar married Beth (Betty) I. Sayre (1925-2014) at Rebecca and David Carbee's home in White River Junction, Vermont. Edgar's parents were, Ernie W. Pierce, born in Canada and Katherine L. Smith, born in Vermont. Emma Mae and Edgar had two children, Ernest Edgar Pierce (Ernie) and Rebecca (Becky) Pierce.

Three Generations

Standing: Edgar Pierce holding Becky Pierce with Fannie and Ernest Shephard. Kneeling, left to right: Emma Mae Pierce holding Ernie Pierce and Charlene Wright being held by Virginia Wright.

Ernest was born July 21, 1940, and married Anita Marie Johnson, on September 5, 1964. Ernest and Anita have three children, five grandchildren, and one great grandchild. Anita was born in Rutland, Vermont, on August 28, 1943. Her father, Gustaf Johnson, was born September 5, 1917 in West Rutland, Vermont, and died May 30, 2005, in Rutland. Her mother was Margaret Liberty, born June 12, 1919, in Rutland, and died February 19, 2007. Gustaf and Margaret were married May 25, 1940, in Rutland.

Rebecca Pierce was born May 30, 1944, in Hanover, New Hampshire, and married David L. Carbee, June 28, 1963. They have three children and eleven grandchildren. David's mother, Frances Reed was born October 25, 1912, in Haverhill, New Hampshire, and died November 18, 1995, in Windsor, Vermont. David's father, Ivo Ladd Carbee, was born July 15, 1908, in West Stewarts Town, New Hampshire, and died January 1981, in White River Junction, Vermont. Both parents were buried in North Haverhill Cemetery in New Hampshire. Ivo Carbee and Frances Reed were married June 4, 1937. Becky said the marriage probably took place in Haverhill, New Hampshire.

Virginia Jane was born August 2, 1919, in Hartford, Vermont, and died March 29, 1999. She married Alfred T. Wright on August 24, 1940, in Hartford. Alfred Wright was born May 26, 1918, in Hartford, Vermont. After Virginia and Alfred were divorced, Virginia Jane married Leopold Madore on June 21, 1957. Leo was from St. Malo, Quebec, Canada. Leo died in Florida about December 2002, and was buried in the Hartford Cemetery. Virginia Jane and Alfred had one child, Charlene Mae Wright.

Charlene Mae Wright was born May 10, 1943, in White River Junction, Vermont. Charlene and Ralph (Peter) Bragg Jr., were married October 21, 1961, in West Lebanon, New Hampshire, and have six children, ten grandchildren, and nine great grandchildren. Peter was born October 22, 1939. His parents were Bernice Hartson and Ralph Everett Bragg. They were married in Fall River, Massachusetts, about 1939.

EMMA A. HANNING AND JAMES CARR

Emma Hanning Shepherd Carr

James Carr was born May 12, 1855, in East Craftsbury, Orleans, Vermont, and died August 15, 1934, at the age of 79, in Bee Branch, Arkansas. James' residence in 1870, was St. Johnsbury, Caledonia, Vermont, living with his parents and siblings doing farming. He married Emma Hanning Shepherd in 1892. In 1900, he was living in Hartford, Windsor, Vermont, with his wife, two daughters, and Ernest A. Shephard, his stepson. He was a blacksmith. In 1910, he was in Bryan, Elko, Nevada, prospecting for gold and was a widower. In 1920, he was back in Spokane, Washington, where he was a blacksmith, living in a boarding house before he returned to Arkansas. James' father was John Carr. He was born in Donaghmore, Ireland, in 1823, and married Agnes Stevenson, February 3, 1854, in East Craftsbury, Vermont. John died January 3, 1892, in East Craftsbury, Vermont, and is buried in the cemetery in Craftsbury. John's wife, Agnes, was born in Scotland, in 1828, and died in Craftsbury, January 3, 1892. James and Emma had two girls, Agnes Carr and Janey Carr.

Agnes was born February 17, 1895, in Lebanon, Grafton, New Hampshire, and died in Duluth, Minnesota, March 24, 1973. Agnes graduated from Hartford High School and became a registered nurse. In the 1920 Census, she was working as a nurse in Newburyport, Massachusetts. After moving to Duluth, Minnesota, sometime in the early 1930s, Agnes, continued her nursing career doing private nursing care in both St. Mary's and St. Luke's Hospital. She never married. Agnes was buried in the Park Hill Cemetery in Duluth Minnesota, in the Bailess Family Plot.

Having lost their mother in 1909, both Agnes and Janey lived with their half-brother, Ernest A. Shephard, in White River Junction, Vermont, until they finished their schooling.

Janey Carr was born November 2, 1896, in Hartford, Vermont, and died February 7, 1978, in Duluth, Minnesota. Janey completed her schooling at the Hartford High School and by the 1920s, she had moved to Duluth, Minnesota, and was a stenographer in the Cargill Grain Office in Duluth. Janey (Jane) and Andrew (Andy) R. Bailess were married in Stambaugh, Iron County, Michigan, July 22, 1929. Andy was born August 26, 1887, in Liskova, Slovakia, and immigrated to the United States, with his family, from Bremen, Germany, March 8, 1897. He came to Minnesota in 1905, and became a naturalized citizen on October 7, 1924. Andy was a machinist and purchased his own business in Duluth in 1931. Andy sold his business and retired in the Fall of 1951. He died April 13, 1969, at his home on Rose Lake, Canyon, Saint Louis County, Minnesota. His parents were Suzanna Krizen Balash and Andrew Balash. Suzanna was born in Austria on September 1, 1864, and died at the Odd Fellows Home in Jackson, Michigan, in 1957. The family lived in Crystal Falls, Iron County, Michigan. After a divorce, Suzanna married Michael (Mike) Chatar Schultz, in Crystal Falls. Suzanna and Mike had one child, Dr. Louis C. Schultz of Ann Arbor, Michigan. Michael was born in Naisal, Austria, on September 7, 1869, and died July 26, 1951, in Jackson, Michigan. Both Suzanna and Michael are buried in the Evergreen Memorial Cemetery in Crystal Falls. Janey and Andy Bailess had two girls, Elizabeth Jane (Betty) Bailess and Susan Frances Bailess.

Betty was born December 23, 1930, in Duluth, Minnesota. She graduated from college in 1952, and received a Master's Degree in Social Work in 1958. She was a Medical Social Worker in various hospitals for ten years before moving to California where she taught and supervised Child Welfare Social Workers for the next twenty-eight years, retiring in 1995. In 1967, she met and later married Bernard Farkas. Bernie was born in Chust, Czechoslovakia, October 23, 1933.

Agnes Carr

Ernest Almon Shephard

Bernie and his mother and father finally arrived in the United States in the early 1940s, after enduring many obstacles, and settled in Chicago where his paternal uncle who sponsored the family lived. Betty and Bernie are now living in Texas, and doing very well. Bernie's parents were Leo and Regina Farkas. Regina was born April 15, 1893, in Sborova, Bohemia, and died August 1984, in Haifa, Israel. Regina and Leo were married July 1932, in Chust, Czechoslovakia. Leo was born September 5, 1905, in Chust, Hungary, and died August 1986, in Haifa.

Susan and Betty Bailess

ABOUT THE EDITOR

I was born in St. Luke's Hospital on August 9, 1934, in Duluth, Minnesota, to Janey and Andy Bailess. I had a happy, normal childhood, starting school when I was five years old. Growing up I was given certain tasks around the house to help Mother with. May 19, 1952, I received a high school diploma from Stanbrook Hall, a preparatory high school affiliated with the College of Saint Scholastica. I received a Bachelor of Science degree from the University of Minensota, Duluth Branch on August 19, 1956, which qualified me to teach elementary grades one through six. I taught in Texas and Florida before moving back to Duluth, Minnesota. On August 20, 1971, I received a Master of Arts Degree, specializing in Reading and Language Arts. Continuing my education, I completed courses needed for licensing in Special Education.

After my marriage to Thorvald Lillevik, on December 26, 1977, I continued teaching for several more years before resigning from my contract.

During this respite from teaching I worked as a "gopher" and "cook" on a Montana farm in the spring and fall of each year as my husband had partial ownership in the farm. I went back to substitute teaching in the Duluth School System in 1994, when our marriage was dissolved, and continued working for five more years in the classroom. I worked as a homebound teacher for three more years, and retired in June of 2002. Since retirement I have done quite a bit of traveling, and when at home, it seems as though I can always find a project. I enjoy sewing, knitting, and many different kinds of needle work; reading, cooking, and taking my little dog for his morning walks. My Schnauzer, Andrej, is now nine years old, and is still a little devil, but he is a real companion and usually a very good boy. This is Andrej's favorite chair where he looks out the window and barks at everyone that walks by. He should have been called "Barker" or "Snoopy."

Editorial Assistant, Andrej

To order additional copies of

An Amazing Journey

Contact Savage Press by
visiting our webpage at
www.savpress.com

or see our Savage Press
Facebook page.

Or call
218-391-3070
to place secure credit card orders.

mail@savpress.com